World Food Café 2

Easy vegetarian recipes from around the globe

World
Food Café 2

Easy vegetarian recipes from around the globe

Chris & Carolyn Caldicott

F

FRANCES LINCOLN LIMITED
PUBLISHERS

Frances Lincoln Ltd
4 Torriano Mews
Torriano Avenue
London NW5 2RZ
www.franceslincoln.com

A catalogue record for this book is
available from the British Library.

ISBN 10: 0-7112-2704-7
ISBN 13: 978-0-7112-2704-0

Edited by Anne Askwith
Designed by Jo Grey
Proofreader Serena Dilnot
Index by Judith Menes

Printed and bound in Singapore
9 8 7 6 5 4 3 2 1

Contents

Pages 1–3
Images of Africa

This page
Top View from Anguilla in the Caribbean; *middle* fruit stall in Rajasthan, India; *bottom* sherbet stall in Hyderabad India

INTRODUCTION

Our first book, published in 1999, was a compilation of the vegetarian recipes we had collected from around the world to serve in our London restaurant, the World Food Café. Although we still serve some of those dishes every day, we continue to travel the world in search of new recipes to introduce to the menu. This book contains the best recipes we have found on those journeys. We visited some places – Cambodia, Guatemala, Belize, Pakistan, Dubai, French Polynesia, Mozambique, Ghana, Tunisia, Jamaica, Anguilla, Nevis and the Maldives – for the first time, and returned to old favourites – India, Sri Lanka, Thailand, Malaysia, Morocco, Kenya, Italy and the Seychelles; and we found delicious dishes in all these places. As before, some of the recipes are for unique vegetarian dishes given to us by people we met on our travels; some are regional variations of traditional dishes typical of a particular country or region; and some are vegetarian versions of local dishes that would normally be cooked with meat or fish.

The traditional cuisine of many countries we travelled in offered plenty of vegetarian dishes, but in others the concept of a meal without meat or fish is anathema. However, as tourists discover more and more remote destinations, hotels and restaurants open to meet their needs, and on some menus vegetarian versions of local dishes that would be impossible to find in local cafés are beginning to appear. Chefs are being recruited from all over the world to new destinations to find ways of using local ingredients and cooking traditions to produce dishes that will satisfy their international guests. Even if it's always more pleasing to find recipes for dishes that are well established in the traditions of an indigenous culture, successful fusions of culinary styles can produce equally delicious results.

The idea of cooking in faraway places food that is just like the food people eat at home, and flying ingredients thousands of miles to achieve it, might seem to rob travel of one of its greatest pleasures, the excitement of discovering new cuisines; there is something strange about eating a meal of Italian pasta in the Maldives, or a Thai curry in the Caribbean. Yet most of us enjoy eating such dishes in our own cities without a second thought.

For centuries, all over the world local cuisines have been constantly changing. Only 500 years ago Europeans had never tasted tomatoes, potatoes, peppers, avocados or chocolate, no one in Asia had ever spiced their food with chilli, no African had grown a field of maize and not a single dish in the Americas had been garnished with coriander or spiced with pepper. So growing rocket in northern Kenya, organic lemon grass in Belize or

The Dadès valley, Morocco

7

Introduction

vines in India is really just an inevitable consequence of ingredients and tastes migrating. Tourism may be the initial impetus that creates a demand for previously unavailable commodities, but in time, some of these will become part of the diet of local people. Nevertheless, there is a danger of the world's cuisine becoming so homogenized that no longer will great voyages of culinary discovery and adventure be possible anywhere.

This seems unlikely in the near future, though, despite certain fast-food chains seemingly being on a mission to offer exactly the same food anywhere on the planet, for most people value variety. And it is still possible to discover local cuisines that have not travelled at all. We recently spent some time in the Apulia region of southern Italy, which is only two hours by air from London, and almost every meal seemed like the best Italian food we had ever tasted, and many of the dishes we ate were probably unknown to most Italians. Eating great food was as memorable a part of the experience of travelling there as the historic cities and beautiful countryside. Just as travel at its best always is.

In Cambodia we discovered that Khmer cuisine offers an amazing selection of dishes and recipes hardly ever heard of outside the country. Even in the most basic street cafés down back alleys or behind markets we ate sensational food. In the chic restaurants of newly opened boutique hotels in Siem Reap and Phnom Penh we ate more sophisticated and inventive versions of the same dishes that were just as delicious. Most Asian countries offer a massive choice of vegetarian food, and it was not hard to find exciting new dishes on our return visits to Thailand and Malaysia.

We have found so many new recipes on recent trips to India that the biggest challenge was trying to limit the number we have included in this book. Pakistan offered some interesting variations of dishes we had eaten before in north India. Travelling there was like being in India thirty years ago: tourists are so rare that they are treated with an almost embarrassing level of hospitality and welcome. From the teeming bazaars of Lahore to the remote hillsides of the Hunza valley, everyone we met was uncompromisingly friendly and seemed genuinely flattered that we had chosen to visit their country.

Sub-Saharan Africa and anywhere in the Americas south of Mexico are the hardest places to find delicious meals that are naturally vegetarian. There are always surprises and exceptions, though. We had a sensational breakfast in Guatemala and the best cauliflower cheese on earth in Belize. Even in Africa we managed to satisfy our taste often enough to never go hungry, especially in Ghana, Mozambique and Kenya.

African countries north of the Sahara offer much more choice for vegetarians. Morocco seems to be able to provide us with a notebookful of new recipes on every visit. This time we went to Fez, which rivals Marrakech as a destination for exotic adventures

Top **Food shop in India**

and fine food. Our first trip to Tunisia provided us with some new styles of Moroccan standards such as harissa and couscous and some new recipes for local delicacies with strange names such as *ojja* and *briq*. As Dubai is a land of souks and Arabic traditions, we have included it in the same chapter as Morocco and Tunisia. Dubai is an extraordinary place. Situated in a desert, it has become a wealthy, modern global village. We met people from every corner of the world living and working there: Brazilian barmen, Burmese gardeners, Indian masseurs, Polish shop assistants, Bangladeshi builders, Philippine nannies, Irish horse owners, American architects and Australian musicians. There were also thousands of tourists. The impressive thing was that all these people of different race, religion and background seem to live together in a small place with almost no conflict or crime.

Islands are often good places to find unusual food. Limited space to grow things, distance from other lands and waves of settlement by completely different peoples can combine to create some unique dishes. There are also some surprising similarities in the cuisine of islands as far apart as the Seychelles and the Caribbean, and some ingredients such as coconut and breadfruit seem to be a part of the diet of every tropical island in the world. In the remote Marquesas Islands of French Polynesia we found some very interesting dishes and a strong sensation of being utterly in the middle of nowhere.

The islands of the Caribbean are close enough to each other for it to be rare to be on an island that doesn't have a view of its neighbour, yet eating habits can change dramatically from one island to another. Jamaica, Anguilla, Nevis and Grenada all provided us with good recipes for local variations of Creole classics. The food of the Seychelles is often described as Creole too and some dishes clearly share the same African roots.

On the other side of the Indian Ocean the islands of the Maldives have no cultural link with Africa. Fish inevitably dominates the local diet, as there is so little land suitable for cultivation. The most interesting food available tends to be based on recipes from the islands' nearest neighbours, India and Sri Lanka. The cuisine of Sri Lanka has always been one of our favourites and our latest visit, this time to the area around Trincomalee on the east coast, provided a bountiful crop of new recipes.

As with the previous book, we have substituted ingredients that would be hard to find with others that are more readily available. We have cooked every recipe both on the large scale we need for the café and in a scaled-down version for cooking at home. As we love spicy food, the quantities of spices reflect the way local people like to eat them. To cook milder versions that are still full of flavour it's easy to reduce the quantity of chilli used. We hope you will enjoy cooking and eating these recipes as much as we do.

All the recipes in the book serve six people, unless otherwise stated.

Bottom Coco pods in West Africa

North Africa and

Arabia

North Africa and Arabia

When Arab horsemen arrived in North Africa in the seventh century, they established Islam as a new religion, built magnificent cities, and introduced exciting new ingredients to be blended with local dishes and sold in the markets. From Dubai to Fez, these market areas or souks – which are to be found in the medina, the heart of every Arab city – are still thriving centres of trade and socializing. They offer a chance to taste local food and experience how similar ingredients can be used in very different ways. As a tourist it's easy to feel like a mere observer, unconnected to these scenes, which could be straight out of *The Arabian Nights*. It's also easy to get lost and, considering the dazzling choice of ingredients on sale, surprisingly hard to find a decent meal.

We found that the best way to taste the traditional cuisine of Fez at its best, and to have a more engaging experience of the souk without getting lost or missing any of the best bits, was to book a day's cookery course. This also presented an opportunity to find some new recipes to use at the World Food Café, many of which are included here.

When we turned up at the home of Abdelfettah Saffar, who introduced himself simply as Fettah, the women of his house were busy dictating him a shopping list of ingredients needed for the dishes we were going to learn how to cook. We were dispatched down alleyways of splintered sunshine into the heart of the medina to haggle our way through the list. With Fettah acting as guide, translator and financial adviser, we slowly filled our baskets with produce. We also bought a hand-made kitchen knife, an earthenware tajine, a pot of lavender honey, a giant jar of multi-coloured olives, several bags of spices, and a brass pestle and mortar to take home.

In Tunis you enter the medina from the elegant French colonial Ville Nouvelle quarter, through the Bab Bhar, a huge arched gateway. The souks beyond it cater specifically for tourists, and are dominated by stalls of stuffed camels and expensive spices in tiny packets. Even here there are plenty of atmospheric cafés serving typical Tunisian snacks such as *lablabi*, a hearty spiced chickpea soup, *mechouia*, a salad of roasted chopped vegetables, and *briq à l'oeuf*, triangles of deep-fried filo pastry with a fried egg inside. Further into the medina we found souks piled high with local produce and restaurants selling Tunisian specialities like couscous and *ojja*, a Tunisian version of egg and chips.

Even in ultra-modern Dubai there is still an old souk along the creek. Although it is almost entirely dedicated to selling gold, there are a few stalls on the fringe selling spices and frankincense. Most of the cafés here specialize in biryanis to cater for the armies of migrant workers from the Indian subcontinent. A few offer the local version of biryani, a pilau of rice with pulses, dried fruit, nuts and seeds served with the popular Middle Eastern spice mix duqqa, puréed beans and rose water-scented salads.

In Fez's ancient medina the merchants of the souk sell mounds of succulent olives, baskets of sweet dates, necklaces of dried figs, pyramids of multi-coloured spices, cartloads of oranges, glistening fish, and fresh vegetables and herbs. Bakers produce trays of warm bread from glowing ovens. Potters' kilns release clouds of black smoke from tall chimneys. Animal skins are draped over the walls of caravanserais and then immersed in a mosaic of pits filled with dyes, from indigo to saffron yellow. Behind secret doorways are opulent palaces and forbidden mosques. Laden donkeys force their way through the throng of locals, many dressed in long robes with hoods drawn over their faces.

Pages 10-11 **A kasbah of Skoura oasis in the Dadès valley, Morocco, the Atlas mountains in the background**

Right **Images of a North African souk**

North Africa and Arabia

In Morocco meals usually start with appetizers of cooked salads, served cold with unleavened bread. Here are a couple of suggestions.

GRILLED PEPPER AND TOMATO SALAD

4 large red peppers
6 medium tomatoes, roughly chopped
5 tablespoons olive oil
3 garlic cloves, thinly sliced
2 red chillies, finely chopped
2 teaspoons paprika

1 teaspoon ground cumin
¼ teaspoon ground white pepper
juice of ½ a lemon
salt to taste
large handful of chopped
    flat-leaf parsley

Grill the peppers until blackened on all sides. Place in a bowl and cover with cling film for 10 minutes; this should make them easier to peel. Peel and dice them.

Blend the tomatoes in a food processor until smooth. Heat the olive oil in a frying pan. When hot, add the garlic and chillies, and fry until brown. Stir in the spices, and then add the blended tomato, cover the pan and gently simmer until the sauce has reduced and the oil has returned. Add the peppers, lemon juice, salt to taste and parsley, and simmer, uncovered, for a further 10 minutes. Serve chilled.

AUBERGINE SALAD

1½lb/750g aubergines, cut into
    quarters lengthwise
5 tablespoons olive oil
4 garlic cloves, thinly sliced
2 heaped teaspoons cumin seeds

3 teaspoons paprika
juice of 1 lemon
large handful of chopped
    coriander leaves
salt to taste

Cook the aubergine quarters in boiling water until soft. Drain and allow them to cool a little before scooping the flesh away from the skin and roughly chopping.

Heat the oil in a frying pan. When hot, add the garlic and fry until brown. Stir in the spices and then add the aubergine. Sauté for a few minutes, add the lemon juice, coriander and salt to taste, and gently simmer for 5 minutes. Serve chilled.

A bedouin with camels in the Dubai desert

DATE, FIG AND CINNAMON TAJINE

6 largish carrots, cut into
    quarters lengthwise

3 sweet red capsicums (the ones that
    look like big red chillies), cut into
    thirds lengthwise

1lb/450g sweet potatoes, peeled and
    cut into 2 × 1in/5 × 2.5cm chunks

1lb/450g butternut squash, peeled and
    cut into 2 × 1in/5 × 2.5cm chunks

12oz/350g Jerusalem artichokes, left
    whole unless large, in which case
    cut down the middle

1 medium red onion, thinly sliced

18 stoned dried dates

18 dried figs

2oz/60g butter, diced

1 teaspoon ground white pepper

1 teaspoon ground ginger

1 heaped teaspoon ground cinnamon

½ teaspoon ground turmeric

good pinch of saffron

1 dessertspoon honey

16fl oz/500ml warm water

salt to taste

2 cinnamon sticks, broken into quarters

3oz/90g almonds, to garnish

2 tablespoons sesame seeds, to garnish

Layer the vegetables, dates and figs in the bottom of a tajine or saucepan, in the order listed in the ingredients, and dot with the butter. Combine the pepper, ginger, cinnamon, turmeric and saffron with the honey and 8fl oz/250ml warm water, and pour over the vegetables. Add salt to taste and the broken cinnamon sticks and 8fl oz/250ml water. Cover the pan, bring to the boil, and then reduce heat to a minimum and gently cook until the vegetables are really soft.

Meanwhile sauté the almonds in a little butter until golden and dry roast the sesame seeds in a small frying pan until golden.

Serve garnished with the almonds and sesame seeds with crusty bread and any of the salads in this chapter.

Traditionally Moroccans cook tajine dishes in an earthenware pot with a tall conical lid designed to capture all the flavours of the spices and infuse them into the ingredients as they slowly cook. These tajines are easily found in every Moroccan market for a few dirhams. They are quite fragile but can be carried home with care. More fancy versions, often gaily painted, can be found in kitchen shops outside Morocco; however, a large thick-bottomed saucepan with a lid will make a good substitute. In nearby Tunisia a tajine is a completely different dish to the Moroccan version, more like an Italian frittata made with eggs and served cold with salad.

CAULIFLOWER, FENNEL AND PEA TAJINE

1 medium cauliflower, cut into
　　large florets
3 medium fennel bulbs, cut into
　　quarters lengthwise
1lb/450g baby new potatoes,
　　cut down the middle
9oz/250g shelled peas, fresh or frozen
9oz/250g shelled broad beans,
　　fresh or frozen
18 green olives
2 garlic cloves, finely chopped
1 heaped teaspoon ground
　　white pepper
2 teaspoons ground ginger

2 teaspoons paprika
2 teaspoons ground cumin
1 teaspoon ground turmeric
large pinch of saffron
4 tablespoons olive oil
16fl oz/500ml warm water
salt to taste
large handful of chopped
　　flat-leaf parsley
large handful of chopped
　　coriander leaves
zest of unwaxed lemon, peeled into
　　½in/1cm strips

Layer the vegetables in the bottom of a tajine or heavy-bottomed saucepan, in the order listed in the ingredients. Add the olives and chopped garlic. Combine the spices with the olive oil and then stir in 8fl oz/250ml of warm water. Pour over the vegetables. Add salt to taste, the chopped parsley and coriander, the lemon zest, and 8fl oz/250ml of water. Cover the pan, bring to the boil, reduce heat to a minimum and gently cook until the vegetables are soft.

Serve with your choice of salad and bread.

POMEGRANATE, BEETROOT AND WALNUT SALAD WITH GOAT'S CHEESE

When you buy cooked beetroot, make sure that it doesn't contain vinegar.

3 Little Gem lettuces, broken into
   separate leaves and washed
12oz/350g packet cooked beetroot,
   cut into cubes and any juice retained
1 pomegranate, cut in half and the
   seeds scooped out
½ teaspoon paprika
½ teaspoon ground cumin
¼ teaspoon ground cinnamon
1 dessertspoon orange flower water

juice of ½ a lemon
3 tablespoons olive oil
1 dessertspoon honey
any juice retained from the
   cooked beetroot
salt to taste
2 handfuls of walnuts
6oz/175g fresh goat's cheese,
   cut into cubes

Arrange the lettuce leaves in a salad bowl, and place the chopped beetroot on top, followed by the pomegranate seeds. Make the dressing by combining the paprika, cumin, cinnamon, orange flower water, lemon juice, olive oil, honey, beetroot juice and salt to taste. Pour over the salad and then sprinkle the walnuts and goat's cheese on top. Chill before serving.

Pomegranate, Beetroot
and Walnut Salad with
Goat's Cheese

FENNEL AND ORANGE SALAD WITH ORANGE FLOWER WATER DRESSING

3 Little Gem lettuces, broken into
separate leaves and washed
2 medium fennel bulbs,
very finely sliced
2 large oranges, finely sliced
2 carrots, grated
large handful of finely chopped
flat-leaf parsley, to garnish

For the dressing
juice of ½ a small orange
2 tablespoons lemon juice
2 dessertspoons orange flower water
1 dessertspoon honey
2 tablespoons olive oil
salt to taste

Layer the lettuce, fennel, orange and grated carrot on a large plate. Combine the dressing ingredients. Pour the dressing over the salad and garnish with the chopped parsley. Chill in the fridge until really cold before serving.

SWEET POTATO SALAD

4 tablespoons olive oil
1 red onion, finely chopped
good pinch of saffron
½ teaspoon ground ginger
1lb 4oz / 565g sweet potatoes, peeled
and cut into smallish cubes
1 teaspoon ground cumin
1½ teaspoons paprika

4 tablespoons lemon juice
zest of 1 preserved lemon or zest
of 1 lemon, cut into strips and
then blanched
large handful of black olives
handful of chopped flat-leaf parsley
handful of chopped coriander leaves
salt to taste

Heat the olive oil in a pan. When hot, add the onion and sauté until the onion is soft. Add the saffron, ginger, sweet potatoes and enough water to half cover. Cover the pan and bring to the boil; then reduce heat and simmer until soft. Add the cumin, paprika, lemon juice, lemon zest, olives, parsley and coriander leaves, and salt to taste. Cook until the sauce has reduced. Allow to cool before serving.

Main picture Fennel and Orange Salad with Orange Flower Water Dressing; *left* Orange seller in the Fez souk, Morocco

GLOBE ARTICHOKE AND CHICKPEA COUSCOUS WITH ONIONS, HONEY AND RAISINS

6 globe artichokes, stalks cut away

2 large red onions, cut into
    eighths lengthwise

1 lb 2oz/500g cooked chickpeas

1 teaspoon ground white pepper

½ teaspoon crushed saffron stamens

1 cinnamon stick

2oz/60g butter

2 tablespoons olive oil

8 coriander stalks, tied in a bundle

2 pints/1.25 litres vegetable stock

salt to taste

For the onions and raisins

2oz/60g butter

4 large red onions, thinly sliced

1 heaped teaspoon ground cinnamon

1 teaspoon ground ginger

½ teaspoon ground white pepper

good pinch of saffron

5oz/150g raisins

2 tablespoons honey

4fl oz/125ml water

salt to taste

For the couscous

1lb 2oz/500g couscous

2 tablespoons butter

Globe artichokes are a really sociable food. Once they are cooked, peel away the leaves, dip them in the stock and eat the soft end. When all the leaves have been eaten, carefully remove the hairy bit to reveal the heart, the most delicious part. Have a big bowl on the table to collect all the finished leaves.

The night market in the Djemaa el Fna and the Koutoubia mosque in Marrakech, Morocco

First cook the artichokes. Place them in a large pan, cover with water, bring to the boil and simmer until the leaves easily peel away. Drain and set to one side.

Place the red onions, cooked chickpeas, white pepper, saffron, cinnamon stick, butter, olive oil, coriander stalks, stock and salt to taste in a heavy-bottomed saucepan. Cover the pan and bring to the boil; then reduce the heat and gently simmer until the onions are soft. Remove the coriander and add the cooked artichokes – you may need to transfer to a bigger pan – and simmer for a further 5 minutes or so.

Meanwhile make the onions and raisins. Heat the butter in a large frying pan. When hot, add the sliced onions, reduce the heat and gently sauté until the onions are nice and soft but not too brown. Stir in the cinnamon, ginger, pepper, saffron and raisins, sauté for a minute, and then add the honey and water and simmer until most of the water has disappeared. Season to taste.

Finally make the couscous. Pour the couscous into a large decorative bowl and pour over enough boiling water to just cover it. When the water has been completely absorbed and the couscous is soft, fluff it up with a fork and then stir in the butter.

Make a well in the centre of the couscous with a spoon, pour the chickpeas and stock into the well, and place the artichokes around the edge. Cover the chickpeas with the onions and raisins.

Tunisians love spicy food and harissa is the main ingredient used to provide the heat. It is very different to Moroccan harissa, using caraway seeds and grilled red pepper to add flavour. We make it in advance and store it in the fridge so that we always have it to hand.

HARISSA

1 red pepper

1 tablespoon ground caraway seeds

3 garlic cloves, crushed

2oz/60g dried red chillies, soaked in
    hot water

1oz/30g ground cumin

2floz/60ml olive oil

salt to taste

First grill the red pepper on all sides until blackened. Place in a bowl and cover with cling film for 10 minutes to make it easier to peel. Peel, deseed and dice the pepper. Combine all the ingredients in a food processor until smooth.

Store in the fridge in an airtight container.

OJJA

In this recipe eggs are poached in a harissa, tomato and red pepper sauce.

3 tablespoons olive oil

4 garlic cloves, finely chopped

1 heaped teaspoon paprika

1 heaped teaspoon ground coriander

1 teaspoon caraway seeds

6 tablespoons tomato purée

3 medium tomatoes, diced

3 red peppers, cut in half and then
    thinly sliced

2 onions, diced

24fl oz/750ml water

harissa (above) to taste

salt and freshly ground black pepper
    to taste

6 large free-range eggs

Heat the oil in a wok. When hot, add the garlic and fry until golden. Add the paprika, coriander and caraway seeds, fry for 1 minute and then stir in the tomato purée, peppers, tomatoes, onions and three cups of water. Add harissa and salt and black pepper to taste. Bring to the boil, cover the wok, and then reduce the heat and gently simmer until the peppers are soft. Carefully break the eggs on top of the peppers, evenly spaced apart. Cover the pan and simmer until the eggs are poached.

Remove from the heat and take straight to the table. Serve with fresh baguette or sautéed potatoes to mop up the sauce.

The Tunis medina,
Tunisia

BRIQ À L'OEUF

1lb 2oz/500g potatoes,
    peeled and cubed

3 tablespoons olive oil

4 garlic cloves, finely chopped

1 teaspoon paprika

¼ teaspoon chilli flakes

½ teaspoon ground black pepper

12 black olives, roughly chopped

2 handfuls chopped coriander leaves

salt to taste

6 filo pastry sheets

6 small free-range eggs

wedges of lemon, to serve

Place the potatoes in a saucepan of boiling water and simmer until soft, drain off most of the water, leaving a little to moisten the mashed potato, and mash until smooth.

Heat the oil in a frying pan. When hot, add the garlic, fry until golden and then add the paprika, chilli flakes and black pepper. Stir into the mashed potato with the chopped black olives, coriander leaves and salt to taste. Divide the potato between the filo pastry sheets, placing some in the middle of each sheet. Then make a well in the middle of the potato, carefully break the egg into the well and fold the pastry like a parcel by folding in the sides and then folding the ends under the parcel, so that the thickest pastry is on the opposite side to the egg, moistening the edges of the pastry to seal the parcel. In a frying pan, heat ½cm of sunflower oil. When hot, place the parcels in the oil, two at a time, and fry on both sides for 2 minutes until quite brown. Remove from the pan and drain on a sheet of kitchen paper.

Serve with the lemon wedges and harissa (page 25) on the side.

This is a delicious and unusual snack or appetizer. Filo pastry is filled with potato mashed with olives and coriander and a whole egg. The parcel is then fried and served with a wedge of lemon. The trick with this recipe is to make sure that the egg yolk remains runny without being undercooked.

Pages 26–27, clockwise from top right **Lifeguard on duty in Dubai; three doorways in the Tunis medina; a café in the Tunis souk; a back street of Sidi Bou Said, Tunisia**

Right **Briq à l'Oeuf**

To explore the vast medina of Tunis we chose to stay in the tiny and absurdly picturesque nearby seaside village of Sidi Bou Said. Although the cobbled streets that wind through the whitewashed houses with their blue painted shutters and studded wooden doorways attract coachloads of visitors every day, in the evenings and early mornings we almost had the place to ourselves. Regular commuter trains link the village with Tunis, so every morning after a peaceful breakfast and walk around the village we left for Tunis, just as the crowds began arriving in the village. On the way home in the afternoon we would stop off at the magnificent Roman and Phoenician ruins of Carthage stretched out over a hillside above the sea with great views across the Gulf of Tunis.

A village mosque in Tunisia

LABLABI

This spicy chickpea soup is very popular with Tunisians and is eaten for breakfast, poured on to broken baguette. Don't be put off by the amount of garlic, as cooking it for a long time mellows it.

8 tablespoons olive oil
10 garlic cloves, finely chopped
12oz/350g chickpeas, soaked
    overnight and then drained
1 large red onion, diced
3 carrots, diced
6 celery stalks, diced
1 heaped teaspoon ground cumin
1 teaspoon ground coriander

1 teaspoon paprika
salt and freshly ground black pepper
    to taste
juice of 1 lemon
baguette, broken into chunks
handful of chopped coriander leaves,
    to garnish
harissa to taste (page 25), to serve

Heat half the olive oil in a saucepan. When hot, add the garlic and sauté until golden. Add the chickpeas and enough water to cover them by 1in/2.5cm. Bring to the boil, removing any foam that rises to the surface, and then reduce the heat, cover the pan and simmer until the chickpeas are soft.

Meanwhile heat the remaining olive oil in a wok. When hot, add the chopped onion, carrots and celery, and sauté until soft; it helps if you cover the wok and let the vegetables sweat. Towards the end of cooking, add the cumin, coriander and paprika. Stir the vegetables into the cooked chickpeas, followed by salt and black pepper to taste. Pour half the soup into a food processor and blend until smooth. Return it to the unblended soup, adding more water if necessary, and simmer for a further 5 minutes. Add the lemon juice.

Place baguette chunks, to taste, into the bottom of a soup bowl and pour over the soup. Serve garnished with chopped coriander leaves and harissa to taste.

COUSCOUS SALAD WITH GRILLED RED PEPPERS, TOMATOES AND FETA CHEESE

6oz/175g couscous

2 red peppers, cut in half lengthways

4 tomatoes, cut in half

6 tablespoons olive oil

2 garlic cloves, finely chopped

1 medium aubergine, cubed

2 courgettes, cubed

1 bunch of spring onions, sliced

large handful of chopped
  coriander leaves

handful of chopped mint leaves

3 tablespoons lemon juice

salt and freshly ground black pepper
  to taste

6oz/175g feta cheese, crumbled

Place the couscous in a bowl and pour over just enough boiling water to cover it. When the water has been absorbed and the couscous is soft, fluff it with a fork.

Grill the red peppers and tomatoes until blackened; then remove from heat and allow to cool a little. Peel the red peppers, remove the seeds and cut into cubes. Cut the tomatoes into cubes. Meanwhile heat half the oil in a wok. When hot, add the garlic and sauté until golden. Add the aubergine and courgettes and fry until soft.

Combine all the ingredients in a large bowl except the feta, and then sprinkle the feta over the top. Serve the couscous warm or chilled from the fridge.

DUQQA

Duqqa is a spice mix used throughout the Middle East as a condiment — it is found on the table along with salt and pepper. We usually make it in advance and store it in our spice cupboard.

1 heaped tablespoon coriander seeds
1 heaped tablespoon cumin seeds
1 heaped tablespoon sesame seeds

Dry roast the ingredients in a small frying pan until they are aromatic, remove from the heat and grind to a powder. Store in an airtight container.

If you learn only one word of Arabic in Fez, it should be *barek*, meaning look out. It's a word you will hear often and a warning you will ignore at your peril. The medina of the old city, Fes el-Bali, is a labyrinth of over 9,000 winding lanes and alleyways between bazaars, mosques, *medersas* (Islamic colleges), souks, old caravanserais (lodges), hammams (baths), tanneries, bakeries, palaces and riads. Fighting their way between the pedestrians who crowd these narrow passages are determined donkeys pulling carts laden with improbable loads. To locals, a shout of '*Barek*' from a donkey driver is the cue for a mass shift to the side. For the tourist, distracted by the sights of the medina or engrossed in framing the perfect photograph, such moments are dangerous. The donkeys wear rubber shoes made of old tyres to help them grip on the steep gradients, so you don't hear them coming. Being tuned in for calls of '*Barek*' is your only chance.

In Fez I asked a guide for help in finding a Moroccan kitchen knife to buy for my cookery lesson the following day. We set off down a quiet alleyway that led eventually to a dead end and an old wooden door. The guide knocked on the door. It was slowly opened by an old woman who let us in with a look that suggested that she had played her role in this trick before. We climbed some stairs, which came out on to a flat roof. On the far side another doorway led down into a carpet shop and out on to another street in a completely different part of the medina. In the knife grinders' souk, men in cavernous workshops powered huge wheels of stone with their feet as sparks flew from their metal blades.

WHITE BEAN AND MINT PURÉE WITH DUQQA

10oz/300g white butter beans
2 garlic cloves, roughly chopped
4 tablespoons olive oil
juice of 1 lemon
large handful of chopped mint leaves

salt and freshly ground black pepper
   to taste
olive oil, to serve
duqqa (page 32), to serve

Blend all the ingredients, except the duqqa, with a little water, in a food processor until smooth. Pour into a bowl and chill in the fridge.

Before serving, drizzle with some extra olive oil and sprinkle with as little or as much duqqa as desired. Serve with Rocket and Orange Salad with Rose Water Dressing (below).

ROCKET AND ORANGE SALAD WITH ROSE WATER DRESSING

salad bowl of rocket leaves
3 medium oranges, peeled and sliced
large handful of coriander leaves
juice of ½ an orange

1 tablespoon rose water
3 tablespoons olive oil
salt and freshly ground black pepper
   to taste

Add the sliced oranges to the rocket and sprinkle over the coriander. Combine the orange juice, rose water, olive oil and salt and pepper to taste, and pour over the salad. Chill until ready to serve.

CHICKPEA, DATE AND PINE NUT PILAU

Pilau is a mixture of pulses, dried fruit, nuts or seeds, spices and rice. It is traditionally made with white rice; however, we prefer to make it with brown.

5oz/150g dried green lentils, soaked in water overnight	1oz/30g pumpkin seeds
4 teaspoons coriander seeds	2oz/60g raisins
1in/2.5cm piece of cinnamon	3oz/90g dates, cut into small pieces
8 cloves	10 oz/300g cooked brown rice
½ teaspoon ground cardamom	12oz/350g cooked chickpeas
2 tablespoons olive oil	5fl oz/150ml vegetable stock
2oz/60g butter	2 large handfuls of flat-leaf parsley, chopped
1 large red onion, sliced	handful of mint leaves, chopped
3 medium carrots, cut into small cubes	salt and freshly ground black pepper to taste
2oz/60g pine nuts	

Cook the soaked green lentils in boiling water until soft, drain and set to one side.

Meanwhile dry roast the coriander seeds, cinnamon, cloves and cardamom in a small frying pan until aromatic, remove from the pan and grind to a powder. Heat the olive oil and butter in a wok. When hot, add the sliced onion and carrots, and sauté until soft. Add the pine nuts, pumpkin seeds, raisins and dates, and fry until the pine nuts are golden. Stir in the spices and fry for 1 minute. Then add the cooked lentils, cooked brown rice, cooked chickpeas and vegetable stock. Bring to the boil, cover the wok and gently steam until all the stock has been absorbed. Finally stir in the chopped parsley and mint leaves, and season with salt and pepper to taste.

Serve with White Bean and Mint Purée with Duqqa (page 35) and Rocket and Orange Salad with Rose Water Dressing (page 35).

Chickpea, Date and
Pine Nut Pilau

Sub-Saharan

Africa

Counting stars by candlelight was a romantic start to a memorable night. The star beds of Loisaba offer a chance to enjoy an unobscured view of the equatorial sky of East Africa from the safety of a comfy bed on a high wooden platform deep in the Kenyan bush. For anyone with a passion for the vast and subtle celestial intrigues of the night sky, this is the ultimate stargazing experience.

The heavenly spectacular ended as a deep orange glow behind the hills on the horizon faded to release the sun into another cloudless blue sky. A Samburu youth, wrapped in a traditional deep orange blanket, emerged through the platform's trap door, offering a welcome pot of morning tea.

Our tour of East African wilderness lodges offered plenty of visual feasts, from spectacular vistas to meetings with colourfully attired Samburu and Masai villagers and close encounters with wild animals. In terms of finding recipes for local vegetarian dishes the experience was more of a famine. There was no shortage of good food cooked by inventive young foreign chefs recruited from the restaurants of Europe, Australia and South Africa to pamper guests on their safaris, but their recipes were fusions of international influences that had little to do with indigenous cuisine. As most local food was based on thin meat stews and maize meal, the only recipes that really worked for us were dishes that had been influenced by the Portuguese and Indian settlers of the past and integrated into East African cuisine using locally grown ingredients. These included *piri piri*, a spicy sauce in which chillies, which the Portuguese brought from Mexico and began growing in their African colonies, are combined with other ingredients such as garlic and lemon juice. Chilli-based sauces are referred to as *piri piri* all over Africa.

The Portuguese passion for spicing things up with *piri piri* has endured long after the last of the colonists fled Mozambique in the early 1970s as their African empire crumbled into chaos and through the civil conflict that followed and until very recently has kept tourists well away from this part of southern Africa. On the island of Bazaruto off the south coast of Mozambique we ate memorable meals of vegetables marinated in *piri piri* and then barbecued on nighttime beach fires.

The most impressive feature of Bazaruto is the mountainous sand dunes that run along its west coast. Here the sea is rough and too popular with sharks for swimming. It pounds the shore with a force that creates a savage beauty that is best enjoyed by riding one of Indigo bay's six fine Boerperd horses. Between the dunes and the tranquil, supposedly shark-free east coast there are several lakes, some with crocodiles, and villages where dhows are still built by hand.

Pages 36–37 Fishermen hauling in nets on Elmina beach, Ghana

Right, clockwise from top right Coastal dunes on Bazaruto; the back of a Samburu hunter, Kenya; a dhow in the Bazaruto archipelago, Mozambique; a Fulani woman in Djene, Mali; dhow crew, Mozambique; a courtship dance in a Samburu village, Kenya

BAKED SWEET POTATO WITH WEST AFRICAN TSIRE (SPICED PEANUT BUTTER)

This utterly delicious take on baked potato using sweet potatoes and a typical West African style of spicy peanut butter called tsire makes a great simple supper.

6 medium orange-fleshed sweet potatoes	1 teaspoon dried chilli flakes
3oz/90g peanuts, with skins removed	1 teaspoon ground ginger
⅓ teaspoon allspice	½ teaspoon freshly grated nutmeg
2 in/5cm piece of cinnamon	½ teaspoon crushed black peppercorns
8 cloves	½ teaspoon salt
	4oz/115g unsalted butter

Preheat the oven to 400°F/200°C.

Bake the sweet potatoes for about 1 hour, until soft.

Meanwhile make the tsire. Dry roast the peanuts in a small frying pan until brown on all sides, remove from the pan and allow to cool. In the same pan, dry roast the allspice, cinnamon and cloves until aromatic, remove from the pan and grind to a powder. Combine with all the remaining ingredients except the butter and blend in a food processor until finely chopped. Gently melt the butter in a saucepan and stir in the spice mix. Cook for a couple of minutes and then remove from the heat.

Cut open the potatoes and spoon in the spiced butter. Serve immediately.

EAST AFRICAN PIRI PIRI

8 large red chillies, roughly chopped	1 teaspoon salt
4 garlic cloves	3fl oz/100ml lemon juice
2 teaspoons paprika	4fl oz/125ml olive oil
1 teaspoon ground black pepper	

Blend all the ingredients in a food processor until smooth. Store in the fridge in an airtight container.

The East African version of *piri piri*, the chilli-based sauce made all over Africa, is not as hot as the original Portuguese version made in Mozambique. This *piri piri* works well as a barbecue marinade or as a condiment. We make a jarful and store it in the fridge.

In Mozambique *piri piri* is served with absolutely everything. It is much more fiery than the *piri piri* found in other parts of Africa, so use it sparingly; and it is made with green chillies and fresh coriander, so it is green instead of red. As it is quite hot, this recipe yields less than regular *piri piri*.

MOZAMBIQUE PIRI PIRI

1oz / 30g thin green chillies
2 teaspoons crushed garlic
1 shallot, diced
3 tablespoons olive oil

3 tablespoons sunflower oil
3 dessertspoons lemon juice
handful of chopped coriander leaves
salt to taste

Blend all the ingredients in a food processor until smooth. Store in the fridge in an airtight container.

A natural rock pool in northern Kenya

EAST AFRICAN WILDERNESS SWEET POTATO PATTIES

We enjoyed these sweet potato patties, served with mixed leaves and mung bean sprouts, as a snack after a game drive.

10oz/300g sweet potatoes, peeled and cut into cubes

10oz/300g white potatoes or yam, peeled and cut into cubes

2 teaspoons cumin seeds

2in/5cm piece of cinnamon

6 cloves

½ teaspoon ground turmeric

½ teaspoon cayenne pepper

½ teaspoon ground cardamom

2 tablespoons sunflower oil

1 medium onion, diced

1 small red pepper, diced

4oz/115g sweet corn kernels, fresh or frozen

1 tablespoon grated ginger

good knob of butter

1 small egg, beaten

handful of coriander, finely chopped

salt and freshly ground black pepper to taste

Place the potatoes in a saucepan of boiling water and simmer until soft.

Meanwhile dry roast the cumin seeds, cinnamon and cloves in a small frying pan until aromatic, remove from pan and grind to a powder. Combine with the remaining spices. Heat the oil in a wok. When hot, add the onion and pepper, and fry until soft. Add the sweet corn and ginger, sauté for a couple of minutes, and then stir in the spice mix; fry for 1 minute and then remove from the heat.

Drain the potatoes and mash, with the knob of butter, until smooth; then stir in the spice and vegetable mix, the beaten egg, chopped coriander and salt to taste. Shape the mixture into patties and fry in a non-stick pan with a little sunflower oil until brown on both sides.

Serve with East African Piri Piri (page 40), mixed leaves and mung bean sprouts.

You can use *piri piri* to add spice to any meal or mix it with extra oil and lemon to make a marinade. Any combination of vegetables or ingredients such as tofu, tempeh or halloumi cheese, marinated in the East African Piri Piri on page 40 and then cooked on a barbecue, will make a memorable meal.

East African Wilderness Sweet Potato Patties with East African Piri Piri

KENYAN CURRY WITH OKRA AND PEAS, TOPPED WITH A FRIED EGG

There are obvious Indian influences in this recipe. Indians have been living in East Africa so long that it has become a local dish, using the popular African vegetable okra.

1 medium onion, roughly chopped
2 garlic cloves, roughly chopped
thumb-sized piece of ginger, peeled
    and roughly chopped
3 red chillies, roughly chopped
4 medium tomatoes, roughly chopped
2 teaspoons coriander seeds
1 teaspoon cumin seeds
2 teaspoons mustard seeds
1 teaspoon fennel seeds
½ teaspoon fenugreek seeds
1in/2.5cm piece of cinnamon
½ teaspoon ground turmeric

1 teaspoon paprika
4 tablespoons sunflower oil
1 medium onion, sliced
13oz/375g baby new potatoes,
    cut into chunks
5oz/150g okra, whole
5fl oz/150ml water
3 bay leaves
6oz/175g shelled peas, fresh or frozen
salt to taste
6 free-range eggs
chopped coriander leaves, to garnish

Blend the chopped onion, garlic, ginger, chillies and tomatoes in a food processor until smooth.

Make the spice mix by dry roasting the seeds and the cinnamon stick in a small frying pan until aromatic. Remove from the heat and grind to a powder. Combine with the turmeric and paprika.

Heat the oil in a wok and when hot add the sliced onion and fry until it starts to soften. Add the potatoes and okra, and fry until the potatoes start to brown, stirring regularly. Stir in the spice mix and fry for a couple of minutes. Add the blended onion, garlic, ginger, chillies, tomatoes, water and the bay leaves, and bring to the boil. Cover the wok and gently simmer until the potatoes are soft and the sauce has reduced. Add the peas and salt to taste and cook for a further 5 minutes.

Break the eggs into a non-stick frying pan and fry with a little oil, until cooked with a soft yolk.

Garnish the curry with the chopped coriander leaves and serve, topping each portion with a fried egg.

Samburu tribesman, northern Kenya

45

India

F inding recipes for great vegetarian dishes in India is never a problem
Regional variations of ingredients and cooking styles mean that there is no
such thing as typical Indian cuisine.

Hyderabad, the old Islamic capital of south India, is often ignored by tourists
but it is well worth a visit. The bazaars of the old town around the impressive
Charminar mosque are packed full of pearls, bangles, fabrics and huge pots for
cooking biryanis. There are exquisite Islamic tombs of Mughal rulers, elegant merchants' houses and, outside the city, the ruins of Golconda, one of India's finest
forts. The city's cuisine is dominated by complex biryanis that reflect the sophisticated, delicate tastes of its Mughal past. Beyond the city, much of rural Andhra
Pradesh is engaged in tobacco production. For generations the villagers who work
in the fields have had a habit of chewing tobacco, and as a consequence many have
damaged their taste buds. To compensate, local cuisine is heavily spiced. On our
drives through the countryside we ate the hottest food we have ever had in India.

In Rajasthan the combination of dramatic desert landscapes, the bright
colours of Rajput turbans and saris, and the wealth of historic buildings is a seductive mixture. We travelled by car from Udaipur in the south to Jaipur in the north,
staying in a collection of 'heritage hotels'. Some of these were rural palaces that
are still the homes of families descended from the royal rulers who built them.
Others were once the homes of wealthy merchants in cities and one was a tented
camp in the middle of a working farm. We ate some sensational food, including
some unique dishes that were the old family recipes of our hosts.

In Amritsar, every day a vegetarian feast is served free to pilgrims visiting
the Golden Temple of the Sikhs. Up to 30,000 people a day are fed by an army of
volunteers engaged in a mass catering operation on an awesome scale. Such gen-
erosity is typical of the welcome Sikhs offer visitors to their holiest shrine. The
temple complex is a good reason to visit Amritsar, especially at sunset, when the
golden domes of the Hari Mandir Sahib are reflected in the tranquil Pool of Nectar
that surrounds it. From here we travelled by road up into the hill stations and
villages of the Himalayas. In roadside dharbas we ate plenty of wholesome dhal
and some interesting vegetable dishes such as spicy mashed pumpkin.

In Calcutta we went in search of restaurants serving traditional Bengali dishes.
These are surprisingly rare. The local Bengalis spend hours socializing in tea houses
but eat at home, and most of Calcutta's restaurants cater for migrants into the city
who don't have extended families there to provide home-cooked feasts for them.

Pages 46–47 **View over Lake Pichola from the lake palace in Udaipur, Rajasthan**

Right, clockwise from top right **A girl from a nomadic clan in the Shekhawati region of Rajasthan; a village man, Rajasthan; a girl at the tomb of the Qutb Shahi kings of Hyderabad; a Rajput man in Shekhawati; a flower seller in a Calcutta bazaar; a picture in the window of a photographer's shop in Calcutta**

KICHURI

6 cups water

8oz/225g basmati rice

8oz/225g mung dhal, dry roasted in
    a frying pan until golden brown

2in/5cm piece of ginger, peeled
    and grated

2 teaspoons ground coriander

1 teaspoon ground turmeric

½ teaspoon chilli powder

2 teaspoons ground cumin

2 teaspoons jaggery or brown sugar

9oz/250g cauliflower, cut into florets

7oz/200g potatoes, cubed

6oz/175g mooli (white radishes),
    peeled and cubed

5oz/150g shelled peas, fresh or frozen

4oz/115g shallots, peeled and left whole

6 green chillies, slit down the side

salt to taste

4in/10cm piece of cinnamon, broken
    into smaller pieces

6 cloves

6 green cardamom pods

3oz/90g ghee or butter

6 dry red chillies

4 bay leaves

1 large red onion, thinly sliced

2oz/60g raisins

extra ghee or butter

chopped coriander leaves, to garnish

8floz/250ml yoghurt, whisked with
    ¼ teaspoon ground black pepper
    and ¼ teaspoon ground cardamom,
    to serve

hard-boiled egg, quartered, to
    garnish (optional)

Bring the water to boil in a large pan, add the rice and dry roasted mung dhal, cover the pan and gently simmer until the rice is half cooked.

Mix the ginger, coriander, turmeric, chilli powder and cumin with a little water to make a paste and add to the rice and dhal along with the jaggery or brown sugar. Add the vegetables and green chillies and salt to taste, and continue to cook, covered with a lid, until the vegetables are soft.

Meanwhile dry roast the cinnamon, cloves and cardamom in a small frying pan until aromatic and then grind to a powder. Heat the ghee or butter in a frying pan. When hot, add the red chillies and bay leaves and fry for 1 minute. Add the sliced red onion and raisins and fry until golden brown. Add the ground spice mix, fry for 1 minute and then stir into the cooked kichuri.

Serve with extra melted ghee or butter poured over the top – as much or as little as you like – and garnish with chopped coriander. Serve with yoghurt whisked with black pepper and cardamom, and garnished with hard-boiled egg if desired.

Kichuri is traditionally eaten during the monsoon, when villages get cut off and have to rely on rice and dhal, which are always kept in the store cupboard. Kichuri means a mixture, so you can add any vegetables you like. It is also served with boiled eggs; we love it with Egg Curry (page 53).

Jaggery or gur, made of date palm sap, is often used as a sweetening agent in Indian cookery

The Indian version of pizza, uttapam is a wheat-free pancake, eaten for breakfast or mid-morning with chutney. You can improvise with toppings and fillings, but traditionally it is served with diced tomatoes, onion, chilli and coriander. The batter is usually left to ferment at room temperature for a minimum of 3 hours, but the cheat's method is to add baking powder.

MUSTARD SPICED CAULIFLOWER

3 tablespoons black mustard seeds	2lb/900g cauliflower, cut into small florets
3 tablespoons yellow mustard seeds	
6 tablespoons mustard oil or sunflower oil	1 teaspoon ground turmeric
	12fl oz/375ml water
2 teaspoons nigella seeds	6 green chillies, slit down one side
	salt to taste

Grind the mustard seeds to a powder and set to one side.

Heat the oil in a wok. When hot, add the nigella seeds. When they crackle, add the cauliflower and fry until golden brown. Add the turmeric and ground mustard seeds along with the water, chillies and salt to taste. Bring to the boil then reduce heat, cover pan and gently simmer until all the water has evaporated.

Serve with rice, Pumpkin with Chickpeas and Panch Phoran (page 62) and Tomato Chutney (page 62).

UTTAPAM

5oz/150g rice flour	3 medium tomatoes, finely chopped
3oz/90g urad dhal flour	1 red onion, finely chopped
1oz/30g fenugreek seeds, ground to a powder	2 large handfuls of finely chopped coriander leaves
1 heaped teaspoon baking powder	3 green chillies, finely chopped
1 teaspoon sugar	sunflower oil for frying
1 teaspoon salt	butter, to spread on top

Combine the flours, ground fenugreek seeds, baking powder, sugar and salt. Gradually add enough water to make a thick batter, making sure that there are no lumps. Add the chopped tomato, red onion, coriander and green chillies. Heat a little oil in a non-stick frying pan. When hot, pour in a ladleful of batter, using the back of the ladle to spread the batter into a pancake approximately 8in/20cm in diameter. When bubbles form and the batter has set, turn the uttapam and cook the other side.

Serve spread with butter and with Coconut Chutney (page 59) on the side.

EGG CURRY

Several of the recipes in this chapter, like this fantastic egg and potato curry, are vegetarian versions of dishes we found in our favourite restaurant in Calcutta called Kewpie's. The restaurant is so casual and friendly that eating there feels like being a guest at a dinner party with a Bengali family. The restaurant is named after its founder Minakshie DasGupta, known to all as Kewpie. Today her daughter Pia Promina makes sure that each dish leaves the kitchen just as her mother would have cooked it.

1 onion, roughly chopped

2 garlic cloves, roughly chopped

1in/2.5cm piece of ginger, peeled and roughly chopped

2 teaspoons ground turmeric

½ teaspoon chilli powder

6 free-range eggs, hard-boiled

1lb/450g potatoes, peeled and cubed

4 tablespoons sunflower oil

1in/2.5cm piece of cinnamon, broken into small pieces

6 green cardamom pods, crushed

6 cloves

4 bay leaves

1 red onion, thinly sliced

3 tomatoes, finely chopped

12 fl oz/375ml water

1 teaspoon jaggery or brown sugar

salt to taste

Blend the roughly chopped onion, garlic, ginger, turmeric and chilli powder in a food processor until smooth, and set to one side.

Peel the eggs, slash the whites of the eggs a few times, and cut in half. Heat the oil in a wok and when hot, add the eggs and fry until golden. Remove from the pan and set to one side. Add the potatoes to the same pan and fry until brown; then remove from the pan and set to one side.

Add the cinnamon, cardamom, cloves and bay leaves to the remaining oil and fry for a minute or so. Add the sliced red onion, fry until soft and then add the onion spice mix and sauté for 5 minutes, stirring regularly to prevent sticking. Add the chopped tomatoes and fry for a further 5 minutes. Add the water, jaggery or brown sugar and salt to taste, bring to the boil, and then reduce heat. Add the eggs and potatoes, and gently simmer until the sauce has reduced and the potatoes are nice and soft.

Egg Curry

METHI ALOO

Potatoes cooked with fenugreek leaves and yoghurt make a great combination. Fenugreek leaves are sold very cheaply, in big bunches, in Indian stores. You can also buy fenugreek dried, although it's not as good as fresh.

1lb 10oz/750g potatoes,
   peeled and cubed

1 medium onion, roughly chopped

5 garlic cloves

thumb-sized piece of ginger, peeled
   and roughly chopped

4 green chillies, chopped

2oz/60g ghee or butter

8 green cardamom seeds, crushed

6 cloves

2in/5cm piece of cinnamon

2 bay leaves

½ teaspoon fenugreek seeds

1 medium onion, thinly sliced

1 teaspoon ground coriander

½ teaspoon ground cumin

½ teaspoon ground turmeric

4oz/115g natural yoghurt

6oz/175g fresh fenugreek, roughly
   chopped, or 1oz/30g dried fenugreek

8fl oz/250ml water

salt to taste

Place the potatoes in a saucepan of boiling water and parboil until nearly soft, drain and set to one side.

Blend the roughly chopped onion, garlic, ginger and chillies in a food processor until smooth. Melt the ghee or butter in a wok, and then add the cardamom, cloves, cinnamon, bay leaves and fenugreek. Heat until they start to crackle. Add the sliced onion and sauté until the onion starts to brown. Stir in the ground coriander, cumin and turmeric, followed by the potatoes and the onion paste mix, and fry, stirring constantly for 3 minutes. Add the yoghurt, fenugreek and water, bring to the boil, cover the pan, reduce the heat and gently simmer until the potatoes are soft and the sauce is reduced. Add salt to taste.

Serve with Whole Green Chillies in Tamarind and Brazil Nut Sauce (opposite).

A tea picker in Darjeeling

WHOLE GREEN CHILLIES IN TAMARIND AND BRAZIL NUT SAUCE

The amount of chillies in this recipe may look scary, but the large, almost pepper-like green chillies used, available in Indian and Middle Eastern stores, are not spicy.

12oz/350g large green chillies
2 tablespoons desiccated coconut
8 brazil nuts, roughly chopped
2 dessertspoons sesame seeds
4 tablespoons sunflower oil
1 large red onion, finely sliced
1 heaped teaspoon cumin seeds
1 heaped teaspoon ground coriander
½ teaspoon ground chilli
½ teaspoon ground turmeric
3 garlic cloves, crushed
3in/7.5cm piece of ginger, peeled
    and grated
10 curry leaves
14fl oz/425ml tamarind water
    (2 teaspoons tamarind paste
    dissolved in 1¾ cups water)
salt to taste

Boil the whole chillies in salted water until their colour changes and then drain and set to one side.

Dry roast the desiccated coconut, brazil nuts and sesame seeds in a small frying pan until toasted. Remove from the heat and grind to a powder.

Heat the sunflower oil in a wok. When hot, add the sliced onion and fry until golden brown. Stir in the cumin seeds, followed by the coriander, chilli and turmeric. Add the garlic and ginger and the nut and seed paste, and sauté for a few minutes. Add the chillies and the curry leaves, stir into the spices, and then pour in the tamarind water and salt to taste. Cover the pan and simmer for a further 5 minutes.

Serve with either Methi Aloo (page 54) or Hyderabadi Kacchi Biryani (page 56).

HYDERABADI KACCHI BIRYANI

1lb/450g basmati rice

salt to taste

6 tablespoons ghee or butter

2oz/60g raisins

3oz/90g whole almonds

3 medium onions, thinly sliced

3 garlic cloves, crushed

2in/5cm piece of ginger,
    peeled and grated

2 teaspoons chilli powder

1 teaspoon ground turmeric

1lb 5oz/600g peeled and cubed pumpkin

4oz/115g unsulphured dried apricots,
    cut into quarters

salt to taste

¾ cup water

14fl oz/425ml natural yoghurt, beaten

large handful of mint leaves, chopped

large handful of coriander leaves,
    chopped

2 tablespoons lemon juice

2 pinches of saffron, dissolved in 3
    tablespoons warm milk

For the pumpkin masala spice mix

3in/7.5cm piece of cinnamon

6 green cardamom pods

6 cloves

2 bay leaves

1 teaspoon caraway seeds

For the rice masala spice mix

2in/5cm piece of cinnamon

6 green cardamom pods, crushed

6 cloves

Dry roast the pumpkin masala spice mix in a small frying pan. When it becomes aromatic, remove from the pan and grind to a powder.

Wash the basmati rice before putting it in a saucepan with enough water to cover the rice by 1in/2.5cm. Add the rice masala spice mix and salt to taste. Cover the pan, bring to the boil and then reduce heat and simmer until the rice is three-quarters cooked. Remove the pan from the heat, drain the rice and set to one side.

Heat one-third of the ghee or butter in a frying pan. When hot, add the raisins and the almonds, sauté until toasted and then remove with a slotted spoon and combine with the rice. Add the sliced onions to the frying pan, cook until crisp and brown, and set to one side.

Heat the remaining ghee or butter in a heavy-bottomed casserole dish with a tight-fitting lid. Remove half and set to one side. Add the garlic and ginger and fry for a couple of minutes, and then stir in the chilli and turmeric, followed by the pumpkin, chopped apricots and salt to taste. Add the water and a quarter of the

Sikh volunteers cooking free food for pilgrims at the Golden Temple, Amritsar

yoghurt, and gently simmer for 5 minutes.

Now assemble the biryani. Layer half the fried onions and half the chopped mint and coriander leaves over the pumpkin, followed by half the rice. Pour over the remaining yoghurt, mint and coriander. Cover with the remaining rice, onions, lemon juice, melted ghee or butter and saffron milk. Cover the casserole with the lid and cook on a high heat for 3 minutes; then reduce the heat to a minimum and gently cook for a further 15 minutes.

Serve with Whole Green Chillies in Tamarind and Brazil Nut Sauce (page 55).

CHANNA DHAL

This is a dhal made from split chickpeas and tempered with fried fresh coconut and raisins.

8oz/225g channa dhal	2 teaspoons jaggery or brown sugar
3 pints/1½ litres water	salt to taste
1 teaspoon ground turmeric	2 tablespoons ghee or buttter
½ teaspoon chilli powder	¼ small coconut, finely diced
1 teaspoon ground coriander	2 tablespoons raisins, soaked in water
2 teaspoons ground cumin	for ½ hour and then drained
1 teaspoon garam masala	4 bay leaves
6 green chillies, slit down the side	1 teaspoon garam masala

Place the channa dhal in a saucepan with the water and bring to the boil. Remove any foam that rises to the surface Add the turmeric and chilli powder, cover the pan and gently simmer until the dhal is soft. Mash the dhal with a potato masher to break it up a little. Combine the coriander, cumin and garam masala with a little water until a paste forms, and add to the dhal along with the green chillies, jaggery or brown sugar and salt to taste. Continue cooking for a further 5 minutes.

Heat the ghee or butter in a small frying pan. When hot, add the coconut and raisins, and fry until golden. Add the bay leaves and garam masala, fry for 1 minute and pour on to the dhal.

COCONUT CHUTNEY

2½oz/75g desiccated coconut	1 teaspoon black peppercorns,
3 tablespoons chopped ginger	crushed
3 red chillies, roughly chopped	1 teaspoon sugar
4 tablespoons lemon juice	salt to taste
2 teaspoons black mustard seeds	

Blend the coconut, ginger, chillies and lemon juice in a food processor until smooth. Dry roast the mustard seeds and crushed peppercorns in a small frying pan until they pop and then add to the chutney, along with the sugar, salt to taste and enough water to make the chutney moist.

Channa Dhal

KORMA SHAH JAHAN

This recipe was apparently created in the royal kitchen of Shah Jahan, the Mughal emperor who built the Taj Mahal. We make it with paneer, a firm cottage cheese made for cooking and available in blocks from Indian shops and some supermarkets.

Paneer is an unfermented cheese made from milk curd. Uncooked it is quite tasteless, so it is always used in cooked dishes, usually fried in cubes or strips and then added to the dish.

4 red chillies, roughly chopped

1in/2.5cm piece of ginger, peeled and roughly chopped

5 skinless almonds

15 pistachios, shelled

3 teaspoons white poppy seeds

3 dried figs, roughly chopped

4 teaspoons desiccated coconut

4 tablespoons ghee or butter

14oz/400g paneer, cut into cubes

1 medium onion, finely sliced

⅔ teaspoon ground nutmeg

⅔ teaspoon ground cardamom

pinch of saffron

4fl oz/125ml double cream

4fl oz/125ml water

salt to taste

For the garam masala

½ teaspoon cumin seeds

4 cloves

2 bay leaves

4 green cardamom pods

1in/2.5cm piece of cinnamon

6 black peppercorns

½ teaspoon mace

Dry roast the garam masala ingredients in a small frying pan until aromatic, remove from the pan and grind to a powder.

Make the korma paste by blending the chillies, ginger, almonds, pistachios, poppy seeds, figs and desiccated coconut in a food processor until a paste forms.

Heat the ghee or butter in a wok, add the paneer and fry until browned on all sides. Remove from the pan with a slotted spoon and set to one side. Add the sliced onion to the wok and fry until golden brown. Stir in the korma paste, fry for a few minutes, and then add the nutmeg, cardamom and saffron. Add the cream, garam masala, paneer, water and salt to taste. Cover the wok and gently simmer for 4 minutes.

Sikh pilgrims at the Pool of Nectar in the Golden Temple, Amritsar

SPICY MASHED PUMPKIN

1lb 10oz/750g peeled and cubed
  pumpkin
4 dried red chillies
1½ heaped tablespoons coriander
  seeds
4 teaspoons cumin seeds

3oz/90g sesame seeds
1 teaspoon amchoor (dried powdered
  mango)
salt to taste
6 tablespoons ghee or butter
good pinch of asafoetida (hing)

Boil the cubed pumpkin until soft, drain and mash until smooth. Meanwhile dry roast the dried red chillies, coriander seeds, cumin seeds and sesame seeds in a small frying pan until aromatic, remove from the heat and grind to a powder. Add to the mashed pumpkin, along with the amchoor and salt to taste. Melt the ghee or butter in a small frying pan. When hot, add the asafoetida and then gradually stir into the mashed pumpkin. Serve with Korma Shah Jahan (page 60).

PUMPKIN WITH CHICKPEAS AND PANCH PHORAN

4 tablespoons sunflower oil

4 red chillies, slit down the side

3 bay leaves

12oz/350g peeled and cubed pumpkin

8oz/225g mooli (white radishes), peeled and cubed

8oz/225g carrots, peeled and cubed

1 teaspoon ground turmeric

½ teaspoon chilli powder

1 dessertspoon ground coriander

2 dessertspoons ground cumin

1 tablespoon finely chopped ginger

6fl oz/175ml water

8oz/225g cooked chickpeas

2 teaspoons jaggery or brown sugar

salt to taste

2 tablespoons ghee or butter

1 teaspoon garam masala

For the panch phoran

½ teaspoon black mustard seeds

½ teaspoon fennel seeds

½ teaspoon cumin seeds

½ teaspoon nigella seeds

½ teaspoon fenugreek seeds

Heat the sunflower oil in a wok. When hot, add the panch phoran ingredients, chillies and bay leaves. When they crackle, add the vegetables and fry until golden. Combine the turmeric, chilli, coriander, cumin and ginger with a little of the water to make a paste, and stir into the vegetables with the rest of water. Add the chickpeas, jaggery or sugar and salt to taste. Bring to the boil; then reduce heat, cover the pan and simmer until the sauce has reduced and the vegetables are soft.

Melt the ghee or butter in a small frying pan and pour over the vegetables. Finally sprinkle the garam masala over the top.

TOMATO CHUTNEY

1 tablespoon sunflower oil

panch phoran (above)

½ teaspoon chilli powder

8oz/225g tomatoes, diced

2in/5cm piece of ginger, peeled and finely chopped

1 tablespoon raisins

2 teaspoons jaggery or brown sugar

salt to taste

Heat the oil in a saucepan and when hot, add the panch phoran. When it crackles, add the chilli powder, followed by the tomatoes, ginger, raisins, jaggery or brown sugar and salt to taste. Cover the pan and simmer until the chutney has thickened.

One of the essential tastes of Bengal is created by use of mustard oil and the spice mixture known as panch phoran or Bengali five spice. The spices – black mustard seeds, fenugreek seeds, cumin seeds, nigella seeds and fennel seeds in equal quantities – are all fried together in oil, into which they release their perfumes. The resulting aroma and flavour is familiar in many vegetable and pulse dishes that accompany the ubiquitous fish dishes of which Bengalis are so fond.

Pumpkin with Chickpeas and Panch Phoran

Even before the British established Calcutta as an international port and the capital of their eighteenth-century Indian possessions, this coast of Bengal attracted traders. Arab dhows arriving on monsoon winds from the Levant brought fenugreek, cumin, nigella and fennel, four spices of panch phoran (page 62). Merchants from Java brought cloves and nutmegs; from the Malabar coast of India came black pepper, turmeric, cardamom and cinnamon. Junks from China delivered ginger and the Portuguese introduced chillies from the Americas. All these flavours have been combined to create one of the most interesting and least exported regional Indian cuisines.

Pages 64–65, clockwise from top right **A lakeside temple at Pushkar oasis; two images of the spa pool at Oberoi Udaivilas in Udaipur, Rajasthan; the Golden Temple in Amritsar; a reflection of the Taj Mahal; the arch of the Charminar mosque in Hyderabad**

Cauliflower and Pea Masala

CAULIFLOWER AND PEA MASALA

As this is a dry curry, it is important to fit a lid on the wok while the cauliflower cooks, so that it is almost steamed.

7 tablespoons ghee or butter	11oz/325g shelled peas, fresh or frozen
4 whole dried red chillies	1½ tablespoons grated ginger
1½ teaspoons black mustard seeds	1½ teaspoons chilli powder
1½ teaspoons fenugreek seeds	7 teaspoons ground coriander
3 teaspoons cumin seeds	2½ teaspoons ground turmeric
1 pinch of asafoetida	1½ teaspoons ground cardamom
1lb 6oz/625g cauliflower,	4fl oz/125ml water
cut into florets	salt to taste

Heat the ghee or butter in a wok. When hot, add the whole red chillies and fry until they become black. Add the mustard seeds, fenugreek seeds, cumin seeds and asafoetida and fry until they crackle; then add the cauliflower, peas and remaining spices. Add the water, cover the pan and cook on a low heat until the cauliflower is cooked. Add salt to taste.

PRUNE AND DATE CHUTNEY

3oz/90g prunes, roughly chopped	½ teaspoon cumin seeds
3oz/90g dates, roughly chopped	1 teaspoon fennel seeds
3oz/90g raisins	3 red chillies
8fl oz/250ml boiled water	½ teaspoon ground turmeric
1 tablespoon sunflower oil	2 tablespoons honey
½ teaspoon black mustard seeds	salt to taste

Soak the prunes, dates and raisins in the boiled water for 1 hour.

Heat the oil in a small saucepan. When hot, add the mustard, cumin and fennel seeds. When they crackle, add the red chillies and turmeric, followed by the prunes, dates and raisins with the water they have been soaking in. Add the honey and salt to taste and gently simmer the chutney, covered by a lid, until it has reduced.

ROYAL BABY AUBERGINES

½oz/15g peanuts

1oz/30g desiccated coconut

2 teaspoons sesame seeds

4 dried red chillies

2 teaspoons coriander seeds

2 teaspoons cumin seeds

1 tablespoon honey

1 tablespoon chopped coriander leaves

1in/2.5cm piece of ginger,
  peeled and chopped

2 teaspoons ground turmeric

3 garlic cloves

1 teaspoon garam masala

salt to taste

1lb 2oz/500g baby aubergines

5 tablespoons sunflower oil

1 small onion, finely chopped

8fl oz/250ml tamarind water
  (1 heaped teaspoon tamarind
  paste dissolved in 1 cup water)

Dry roast the peanuts in a small frying pan until golden, and then add the coconut, sesame seeds, red chillies, coriander seeds and cumin seeds and continue roasting for a few more minutes. Remove from the heat and grind to a powder. Place the powder, along with the honey, coriander leaves, ginger, garlic, turmeric and garam masala, salt to taste and a little water, in a food processor and blend until a paste forms.

Slit the baby aubergines in half, keeping the stem intact, and fill the aubergines with the paste. Smear any remaining paste on the outside of the aubergines. Heat the oil in a wok. When hot, add the aubergines, four at a time, and fry until brown on all sides. Set to one side. In the same oil, fry the chopped onion until golden, add the aubergines and tamarind water, bring to the boil, cover the pan, reduce the heat and gently simmer until the tamarind has reduced to almost nothing and the aubergines are soft.

Serve with Prune and Date Chutney (page 67).

We had one of our most memorable nights in India staying in the tented camp of Chhatra Sagar at Nimaj, on the road between Jodhpur and Jaipur. The family who farm their ancestral land in this remote part of the state constructed a dam to provide irrigation for their fields and they accommodate guests in luxurious tents pitched along the dam wall, overlooking the lake. Staying here gave us the unique experience of sleeping under canvas deep in the Rajasthan countryside. The food served was the best we have ever eaten in India, all organically grown in the fields around the lake and cooked in an open-plan kitchen by the family.

The owner's sister-in-law, who was on cooking duty that night, welcomed us into the kitchen to watch dinner being cooked and learn about some of the delicious recipes. A cheerful bunch of assistants were on hand for the frying, making

PEAS AND SPINACH WITH GRAM FLOUR AND CURD

1 medium onion, roughly chopped

2 garlic cloves

3 green chillies, roughly chopped

2½fl oz/75ml yoghurt, beaten with
   1 cup water

½oz/15g gram flour (chickpea flour)

1fl oz/30ml lime juice

3 dried red chillies, powdered

1 teaspoon ground turmeric

1½ teaspoons cumin seeds

3 tablespoons sesame oil

2 garlic cloves, finely chopped

10oz/300g spinach leaves, washed,
   stems removed and cut into
   ½in/1cm strips

6oz/175g shelled peas,
   fresh or frozen

22fl oz/600ml water

salt to taste

Blend the onion, garlic and green chillies in a food processor until smooth.

Gradually stir the yoghurt and water mixture into the gram flour, making sure that there are no lumps. Add the lime juice, red chillies, turmeric, cumin seeds and blended onion mix.

Heat the sesame oil in a wok. When hot, add the chopped garlic cloves and fry until golden brown. Reduce the heat and allow to cool a little before stirring in the yoghurt and gram flour mixture, followed by the spinach, peas and water. Gently simmer until the sauce thickens, and then stir in salt to taste.

GHEE

A lot of Indian recipes use ghee, a form of clarified butter. It is incredibly easy to make and can be kept in the fridge for some time, so we thought we would include this recipe.

1 block butter, preferably unsalted

Melt the butter in a small pan. When the butter has melted, it will splutter. Reduce the heat and keep cooking until the spluttering stops and the milk solids that have risen to the surface sink. Pour into a container and allow to cool. Store in the fridge.

Pakistan

Pakistan

When the overnight flight from London delivered us to the steamy summer heat of Islamabad at dawn, making the connection with a 0615 flight on a little Fokker Friendship to whisk us up to the Gilgit was only half the uncertainty: if any bad weather is suspected, the flight can be cancelled at a moment's notice and it has even been known to turn back halfway through the journey if the weather closes in, which it often does during the summer monsoon. But our timing was perfect and the sky was clear.

This is one of the most spectacular flights in the world. We could see the Karakoram Highway below, fighting its way through the foothills of Kashmir and then up into the deep valleys of the mountains. The plane flies past Nanga Parbat, the world's ninth-highest peak at 23,347 feet/8,125 metres, which towered above us.

After the sweatbox of the plains, Gilgit was pleasingly cool, the sun reassuringly still warm in the thin clear air. At the 'Foreigners' Registration Booth' a man with a deeply chiselled face and a thick beard dyed red with henna, who looked like a fierce Pathan warrior apart from his warm smile, welcomed us and entered our details in an antique ledger, which looked as though it had been recording the occupations, intentions and mothers' maiden names of travellers for decades.

Our final destination was the Hunza valley, which we reached by jeep along the Karakoram Highway. At Hunza a deep canyon between the mountains opens out into a broad valley and there is a sudden abundance of fertility. Orchards of apricots, apples, pears, mulberries and cherries among terraced fields of wheat and potatoes and wooded glades of deodar or Himalayan cedar are all watered by ancient systems of water channels fed by melting glaciers nestled among the snowy peaks around the valley. Dominating the whole valley are the white walls and wooden pillars of Baltit fort. Arriving there felt like entering a hidden paradise.

The food in Hunza was excellent. Local specialities include lots of *chamus*, apricot juice; *haneetze daudo*, a noodle and vegetable soup with crushed apricot kernels, on one of which I broke a tooth; *burus berakutz*, a cheese and fresh herb filled chapatti spread with apricot kernel oil; and *garma*, a spinach-like vegetable, served with *phitti*, a robust wholemeal bread.

It was during our stay in Hunza that we learnt many of the recipes in this chapter. Others come from Lahore, capital of the Punjab and a city rich in contemporary and historic culture and fine cuisine. Lahore also has a wealth of sensational Mughal-built mosques, fortifications, mausoleums and gardens, and an old city packed with bustling bazaars.

Pages 70–71 **The Hunza valley in the Karakoram mountains of Pakistan**

Right, clockwise from top right **The Badshahi mosque in Lahore; an apple seller in Azad, Kashmir; the Baltit fort of Karimabad; Punjabi boys in Lahore; a farmer in the Hunza valley; a girl in the Rawalpindi bazaar**

LAHORE BUTTER SAAG

This is a great side dish to serve with dhal and chapatti.

2oz/60g ginger, peeled
2¼lb/1kg spinach, washed, stems
   removed and roughly chopped
6 green chillies, slit down the side
1¼ pints/750ml water

1½ tablespoons cornflour
½ teaspoon chilli powder
5oz/150g butter
salt to taste

Roughly chop two-thirds of the ginger and cut the remaining ginger into fine matchsticks. Put the spinach, 3 green chillies, roughly chopped ginger and water in a pan, bring to the boil and gently simmer for 40 minutes. Drain the spinach, retaining the water. Place the spinach in a food processor with the cornflour and blend until it becomes a coarse purée. Return to the pan along with the chilli powder, remaining green chillies, two-thirds of the butter, salt to taste and retained cooking water. Gently simmer for a further 15 minutes.

Meanwhile prepare the tempering by melting the remaining butter in a small frying pan. Add the ginger matchsticks and sauté for 2 minutes. When the spinach is cooked, pour the tempering over the top and serve immediately.

Left The Badshahi mosque in Lahore; *below left* a young vegetable seller in the Lahore bazaar; *below right* three Ismaili women in the Hunza valley

DHAL MAKHANI

Urid dhal, also known as black dhal, is available from Indian stores. The lentils have dark skins and a white interior.

6oz/175g split black urid dhal, soaked overnight

2 pints/1.25 litres water

5 tablespoons red kidney beans, cooked

2½in/6cm piece of ginger, peeled and finely chopped

5 garlic cloves, crushed

4 tablespoons tomato purée

1 teaspoon chilli powder

3oz/90g butter

4fl oz/125ml double cream

salt to taste

Drain the soaked lentils and place in a saucepan with the water. Bring to the boil, cover the pan, and then reduce the heat and gently simmer until the lentils are cooked. Lightly mash with a potato masher and then add the kidney beans, ginger, garlic, tomato purée, chilli powder, butter and salt to taste. Cook for a further 20 minutes. Finally add the cream and gently simmer for 5 minutes.

Serve with Lahore Butter Saag (page 75), rice and chapatti.

Below The Badshahi mosque in Lahore

Right Women off to harvest apricots in the Hunza valley below the Karakoram mountains

Not only is the scenery of Hunza stunning but the people are particularly friendly and hospitable. They are followers of the Aga Khan and the Ismaili style of Islam. Women are unveiled and comfortable about talking to foreigners, including men.

There have been lots of romantic stories about Hunza and how its people live to exceptionally old age in fine health. They inspired James Hilton to write his novel *Lost Horizon* about a lost kingdom of Shangri-La. In reality Hunza's history has been one of tribal conflicts and power struggles to control the trade route between China and the Indian subcontinent. Nevertheless our stay there was one of the closest experiences to visiting a Shangri-La we have found anywhere in the world.

Paneer, Cashew Nut and Hunza Apricot Masala

PANEER, CASHEW NUT AND HUNZA APRICOT MASALA

This recipe uses ajwain, a seed with a thyme-like flavour. You can buy it from any Indian store. First you make a gravy, and then you add this to the paneer and spices.

For the gravy

1lb/450g tomatoes, diced
1 teaspoon grated ginger
2 garlic cloves, crushed
4 green chillies, slit down the side
8 cloves
8 green cardamom pods, crushed
8floz/250ml water
2oz/60g butter
2fl oz/60ml double cream
2 teaspoons honey
½ teaspoon ground fenugreek
1 dessertspoon ginger, peeled and cut into matchsticks
salt to taste

3 tablespoons ghee or butter
2 teaspoons ajwain seeds
1 medium onion, sliced
1in/2.5cm piece of ginger, peeled and finely chopped
15oz/425g paneer, cut into ½in/1cm cubes
3oz/90g cashew nuts
6oz/175g Hunza or unsulphured dried apricots, cut in half
½ teaspoon chilli powder
1 teaspoon ground coriander
2 teaspoons garam masala
large handful of chopped coriander leaves

To make the gravy, place the tomatoes, grated ginger, garlic, chillies, cloves and cardamom in a saucepan with the water, bring to the boil, reduce the heat and then cover the pan and gently simmer until the gravy reduces to a sauce consistency. Stir in the butter, cream, honey, fenugreek, ginger matchsticks and salt to taste, and continue cooking for a minute or so.

Heat the ghee or butter in a wok. When hot, add the ajwain seeds and, when they crackle, add the sliced onion and ginger. Sauté until the onions soften. Add the paneer, cashew nuts and chopped apricots and fry until the paneer starts to brown. Stir in the chilli powder and ground coriander, followed by the gravy. Gently simmer until the gravy coats the paneer. Finally stir in the garam masala and chopped coriander leaves.

Cambodia

Cambodia

Cambodia has emerged from its appalling recent history with a renewed enthusiasm for the traditions of its ancient past, including some very fine Khmer cuisine. Cambodians are now welcoming visitors to the wonderful jungle temples of Angkor in Siem Reap Provence and their capital Phnom Penh without a hint of the cynicism that can so easily creep in to better-worn destinations. You don't even need to haggle with pedallers of the city's cyclo-rickshaws: the fares they charge are so embarrassingly low that when you give them a well-deserved tip they shake your hand in warm thanks. As the volume of tourists increases, the warmth of this welcome may reduce, so now is the perfect time to visit Cambodia. There is a great choice of hotels to suit most budgets and it's still possible to find yourself alone among the ancient temples and grand palaces.

At its height the Khmer kingdom, centred on Angkor, ruled an empire that included most of South East Asia. The Khmer recipes being revived today go back to this time, before chillies arrived in Asia from Mexico. Consequently dishes are much milder than those of most Asian countries.

There are plenty of places to try delicious traditional Khmer food in Siem Reap, the town closest to the ruins of the Khmer kingdom's greatest relics around Angkor wat. Simple and incredibly inexpensive food is on sale from food stalls around the bustling Psar Chas market. In the pavement cafés near by, equally delicious food is served at tables in the open air. Salads are popular starters, made with ingredients such as banana flower blossom, lotus roots, green mango or green papaya, served with finely chopped roasted peanuts and shrimps, and all doused in lively dressings of lime juice, palm sugar and lots of fresh coriander leaves. Wherever you eat it, *amok* – an aromatic dish of chicken, fish or tofu – is a good choice. Many Khmer dishes include fish sauce or fresh-water shrimps but we have adapted our recipes to exclude these.

Phnom Penh is located at the confluence of the Mekong, Tonla Sep and Bassac rivers. The city's social life is concentrated in the cafés, bars and markets along its attractive riverside promenade. Every afternoon, just before sunset, hundreds of hawkers set up stalls along it, selling an extraordinary choice of snacks and fast food to strolling residents. It's hard to believe that so recently, for three years, this charming city was a ghost town, forcibly evacuated by the Khmer Rouge. The residents who survived those terrible years, when a third of Cambodia's population perished, began repopulating the city only twenty-five years ago. It's taken most of that time for it to recover. At last food production and supplies are well established again and the city's cafés and markets thrive once more.

Pages 80–81 Angkor wat at dawn

Right, clockwise from top right An offering of incense at the feet of a Buddha in Angkor wat; a monk at Siem Reap monastery; Ta Prohm temple, Angkor; Buddhist shrine in Angkor; a stone face at the Bayon temple, Angkor; a monk at Angkor wat

AMOK WITH SPINACH AND TOFU

The most essential ingredient in most Khmer dishes is a herb paste known as kroeung, a blend of lemon grass, galangal, rhizome (or lesser galangal), turmeric and garlic. Sometimes shallots or kaffir lime zest are added.

For the kroeung
1 lemon grass stem, thinly sliced
1in/2.5cm piece of galangal, sliced
½ teaspoon ground turmeric
2 garlic cloves, roughly chopped
2 dried red chillies, soaked until soft
    and then roughly chopped (optional)
2 shallots, sliced

For the amok
5fl oz/150ml coconut milk
1 tablespoon dark soy sauce
1 teaspoon palm sugar or honey

1 small egg, beaten
salt to taste
1oz/30g spinach leaves, washed,
    stems removed and sliced
3oz/90g Chinese broccoli, chopped
2oz/60g deep-fried tofu, sliced
    ¼in/½cm thick

For the garnish
1 large red chilli, finely sliced
1 dessertspoon sliced lime leaves
2 tablespoons coconut cream or thick
    coconut milk

First make the kroeung by blending all the ingredients together in a food processor until a paste forms.

Pour half the coconut milk into a bowl and stir in the kroeung, soy sauce, palm sugar or honey, beaten egg and salt to taste; then add the remaining coconut milk. Choose the bowls in which you are going to serve the amok, making sure that they are heatproof, and divide the sliced spinach, chopped broccoli, sliced deep-fried tofu and coconut spice mix between the bowls. Steam the amok in a steamer for 30 minutes. If you don't have a steamer, you can simmer water in a wok, place the amok on a steamer stand in the bottom and cover with the lid.

Remove the bowls from the steamer and garnish with the sliced red chilli, sliced lime leaves and coconut cream or milk.

Amok is an extremely popular steamed curry, served all over Cambodia. Cambodians like it best with fish or chicken but this vegetarian-style version with tofu often appears on menus. Don't bother to deep fry the tofu yourself – you can buy it. The curry is thickened with egg and flavoured with the classic Khmer spice paste *kroeung*. The resulting dish is solid but moist. Although the traditional *amok* does not include chillies, we prefer this dish to be spicy. To make a milder dish, just leave the chillies out of the *kroeung*.

The *amok* is usually then steamed in a banana leaf but we steam it in bowls. We wouldn't recommend cooking this for large groups, as steaming lots of bowls could be a fiddle, so this recipe serves 2 people.

Amok with Spinach and Tofu

KAPI SAUCE

4 tablespoons lime juice

2 tablespoons light soy sauce

1 teaspoon honey

4 garlic cloves, crushed

2 shallots, finely chopped

2 red chillies, finely chopped

½ teaspoon crushed black
 peppercorns

1 tablespoon peanuts, dry roasted
 until toasted and then crushed

Combine all the ingredients and serve.

GREEN MANGO SALAD

This is great as a light meal, appetizer or accompaniment to a main meal.

2 green mangoes, cut into thin strips

6oz/175g shredded cabbage

2 carrots, grated

For the dressing

2 tablespoons sliced shallots

2 garlic cloves, crushed

1 tablespoon finely sliced lemon grass

1 teaspoon finely chopped galangal

1 red chilli, finely chopped

2fl oz/60ml coconut milk

2fl oz/60ml tamarind water
 (1 teaspoon tamarind paste
 dissolved in water)

1 tablespoon lime juice

2 dessertspoons honey

2 tablespoons light soy sauce

For the garnish

2 tablespoons sliced shallots, fried
 until brown

1 tablespoon sliced garlic, fried
 until brown

2 heaped tablespoons peanuts, dry
 roasted until toasted and then
 crushed

handful of chopped coriander leaves

handful of chopped Thai sweet basil
 or basil

Combine the green mangoes, cabbage and carrots in a bowl. In a separate bowl, combine all the dressing ingredients. Pour the dressing over the salad and mix well. Finally sprinkle the garnish ingredients over the top.

A taste for chillies hasn't entirely passed Cambodia by: often a powerful side dish of *kapi*, chillies mixed with honey, soy sauce, garlic and peanuts, is provided, for those who want to spice things up a bit. *Kapi* sauce is a spicy, thin condiment. There are many versions but this is our favourite. If you don't want heat, leave out the chillies.

A window of a monastery in Siem Reap

CAMBODIAN YELLOW CURRY

This is another dish based on the flavour of a kreoung. In this one the added quantity of turmeric lends a distinctly yellow colour to the curry. Pea aubergines are small, round green aubergines available from Thai supermarkets. You can substitute peas if they are not available.

For the kreoung
grated zest of 2 kaffir limes or limes
2 lemon grass stalks, sliced
1 tablespoon sliced galangal
5 shallots, sliced
4 garlic cloves, chopped
3½oz/100g peanuts, dry roasted
   until toasted
1 teaspoon ground turmeric

For the curry
4 tablespoons sunflower oil

1 medium onion, diced
10oz/300g aubergine, cut into cubes
12oz/350g sweet potatoes, peeled
   and cut into cubes
12oz/350g cauliflower,
   cut into florets
4oz/115g pea aubergine
14fl oz/400ml coconut milk
2 tablespoons dark soy sauce
1 dessertspoon honey
8fl oz/250ml water
salt to taste

First make the kreoung by blending all the spice paste ingredients in a food processor until smooth.

Heat the oil in a wok. When hot, add the onion, fry until soft and then add the other vegetables, sprinkling with a little salt to prevent the aubergine from drying out. Fry until the vegetables start to soften, and then add the kreoung, stirring to coat the vegetables with the spice paste. Add the coconut milk, soy sauce, honey, and salt to taste, bring to the boil and then reduce the heat, cover the pan and gently simmer until the vegetables are soft.

Serve with Savoury Pineapple Salad (page 92), rice and popadums.

Cambodian
Yellow Curry

SAMLA SOUP

Samla is thin soup that is served alongside the main meal. Alternatively you can have it, as we do, for supper with tofu — added at the same time as the spinach — and rice noodles on the side.

2 tablespoons sunflower oil
4 garlic cloves, crushed
1¾ pints / 1 litre vegetable stock
1 teaspoon chopped parsley root
2 teaspoons tamarind paste
1 tablespoon dark soy sauce
1 teaspoon honey
1 teaspoon crushed black
   peppercorns
3 carrots, cut into strips

7oz / 200g baby sweet corn, sliced
   diagonally
3 small tomatoes, cubed
6oz / 175g spinach, washed, stems
   removed and sliced
4 spring onions, thinly sliced
handful of chopped coriander leaves
10 sweet basil leaves, chopped
2 red chillies, finely chopped
salt to taste

Heat the oil in a wok. When hot, add the garlic and fry until brown and crunchy. Turn down the heat and allow to cool for a few minutes. Then add the stock, parsley root, tamarind paste, soy sauce, honey and black pepper. Cover the pan and bring to the boil, add the carrots, baby sweet corn and tomatoes, and simmer until the vegetables are just soft. Add the spinach, spring onions, chopped herbs, chillies and salt to taste. Serve as soon as the spinach has wilted.

TEMPEH STUFFED AUBERGINES

This is a recipe from the Cambodian royal household, the cuisine of which includes dishes to celebrate key events during a reign, offerings to the gods and dishes to mark births, weddings and deaths. We use Chinese aubergines, which are thinner and paler purple than regular aubergines. If you can't get them, don't worry: use regular aubergines, but try to pick small, slender ones. Tempeh (fermented soya bean curd) is available from health food or Asian stores; however, if you find it hard to buy, tofu or vegetables work just as well.

For the kroeung
3 tablespoons finely sliced lemon grass
3 teaspoons grated galangal
1 teaspoon finely chopped parsley root
5 garlic cloves, chopped
7 shallots, chopped
4 red chillies, finely chopped
2 tablespoons dark soy sauce
½ teaspoon coarsely ground
   black peppercorns
salt to taste

3 medium Chinese aubergines, cut
   in half lengthways
6 tablespoons cooked Thai rice
6 oz/175g tempeh, finely chopped
2 free-range eggs, beaten
1 dessertspoon vegetarian oyster sauce
3 tablespoons sunflower oil
spring onions, finely sliced,
   to garnish

First make the kroeung by blending all the ingredients in a food processor until smooth.

Blanch the aubergines in a large saucepan of boiling water for 4 minutes. Remove from the pan, dry with kitchen paper and scoop out the centres, leaving enough flesh to keep the shells firm. Chop up the flesh and mix it with the rice, tempeh, eggs, oyster sauce and kroeung, and stuff the aubergines with the mixture. Heat the sunflower oil in a non-stick frying pan. When hot, fry the aubergines, stuffing sides down, over a moderate heat until soft and brown. Carefully turn the aubergines and fry until the other sides are brown.

Serve garnished with the sliced spring onions. Serve with Kapi Sauce (page 86).

Far left Monks at a monastery in Phnom Penh; *left* a huge stone face above a gateway to Angkor thom

SAVOURY PINEAPPLE SALAD

A perfect balance of sweet, savoury and spicy.

10oz/300g fresh pineapple, cut into
    cubes
small handful of chopped Thai
    sweet basil leaves, or basil
small handful of chopped mint leaves

For the dressing
2 garlic cloves, crushed
2 shallots, crushed
2 tablespoons light soy sauce
2 dessertspoons honey
2 red chillies, finely chopped

Mix the pineapple and the chopped herbs in a bowl. In a separate bowl, combine the dressing ingredients. Pour the dressing over the salad and mix well.

PHNOM PENH STIR-FRY WITH HOLY BASIL

3 tablespoons sunflower oil
6 garlic cloves, crushed
2 red chillies, finely chopped
6 shallots, sliced
1 red pepper, sliced
1 yellow pepper, sliced
9oz/250g fine green beans
9oz/250g Chinese broccoli or
    broccoli, chopped

2 tablespoons vegetarian oyster sauce
1 tablespoon soy sauce
1 teaspoon honey
4fl oz/125ml water
9oz/250g bean sprouts
4 large handfuls Thai holy basil,
    chopped

Heat the oil in a wok. When hot, add the garlic, chillies and shallots, and sauté until soft. Add all the vegetables except the bean sprouts and fry for a few minutes. Add the oyster sauce, soy sauce, honey and water, cover the wok, reduce the heat and cook until vegetables are soft but retain some bite. Stir in the bean sprouts and the chopped holy basil, and fry until the basil wilts.

    Serve immediately with Samla Soup (page 90), Kapi Sauce (page 86) and rice noodles.

Phnom Penh is an easy-going capital with a wealth of excellent street markets and exotic temples, one of the best museums in the world just packed with immense antique Buddhas and a royal palace that rivals any in Asia for opulent splendour. The perfect way to end any day in the city is sipping a cold Angkor beer looking out over the Tonle Sap river from the balcony of the Foreign Correspondents' Club of Cambodia on the promenade.

Savoury
Pineapple Salad

Thailand and

Malaysia

Thailand and Malaysia

Thailand and Malaysia have quite different cuisines, despite sharing the peninsula between the Indian Ocean and the South China Sea that links Singapore to Indo-China. In both countries there are plenty of opportunities for vegetarians to eat well. Thailand stands alone in South East Asia as a nation that was never colonized by Europeans. Thai cuisine, though, was revolutionized in the sixteenth century, when Portuguese ships called in at Thai ports on their way to Macau and introduced the Thais to chillies. Like most other Asian peoples, the Thais quickly found an enthusiasm for this new spice which, until Columbus returned to Europe from the Americas, was unknown beyond the lands around Mexico, where it is a native plant. Today there are few Thai dishes that do not include chillies in the recipe.

Thai food is all about fresh ingredients and fast preparation, making it very healthy and tasty. Dairy products are hardly ever used. When ingredients are fried, it's only briefly in a little oil, and there is an emphasis on lots of fresh flavours such as lemon grass, galangal, lime leaves, ginger and sweet basil. Ironically in recent years Thai food has successfully colonized most of the countries in Europe that failed to colonize Thailand. Although many Thai dishes have become familiar to us in high-street restaurants and even pubs, we still found plenty of new dishes. Thai food will always taste better served in a beach café under the palm trees on the shore of the South China Sea or on the elevated verandah of a restaurant on wooden stilts looking out over terraced rice paddies snaking their way between jungle-covered hills along the banks of the Mekong.

Some of the recipes in this chapter, such as the *chu chee* red curry, come from the coast of southern Thailand, where coconut milk is a ubiquitous ingredient; others, such as the vegetables in a lemon grass and herb-scented broth, are from the hills and forests of northern Thailand. There are some dishes, like *pad thai*, that with a little regional variation are found all over the country. The recipes include the amount of chillies with which Thais would make them. Reducing the heat while keeping all the flavour simply requires a reduction of the chillies. As coconut milk plays such a dominant role in other recipes in this book, we have concentrated on Thai recipes that do not include it.

A passion for coconut milk is well established in Malaysian cooking too. In the recipe for Malaccan *laksa*, a fabulous dish that we ate on the island of Pankor Laut in the Malaccan strait, it is an essential ingredient. Kuala Lumpur is one of the street food capitals of the world. Among the thousands of makeshift cafés and stalls that feed the city's residents and visitors we found the recipe for crisp vegetable and coconut salad. We have also included a recipe for sambal sauce, which is an essential accompaniment to any Malaysian meal.

Pages 90–91 **A house on stilts in the Strait of Malacca, Malaysia**

Right, clockwise from top right **Harvesting rice at Dhara Dhevi in Chaing Mai; the roof of a Thai house; a reclining Buddha in Phuket; limestone cliffs at Krabi; a water pot; sandals at Pankor Laut spa village**

TOFU WITH CRISPY FRIED BASIL AND CHILLI SAUCE

This recipe makes a good side dish to Stir-fried Vegetables with Green Peppercorns and Shitake Mushrooms (page 103).

5 tablespoons sunflower oil	3 tablespoons vegetarian oyster sauce
1 cup Thai sweet basil leaves, or basil	3 tablespoons dark soy sauce
14oz/400g tofu, cut into	2 tablespoons chopped palm sugar
½in/1cm slices	or honey
6 garlic cloves, sliced	3 teaspoons cornflour mixed with
6 red chillies, finely sliced	8 tablespoons water

Heat 2 tablespoons of the sunflower oil in a wok. When hot, fry the basil leaves until crispy and set to one side. In the oil remaining in the pan, fry the tofu until brown on both sides. Remove the tofu from the wok and then add the remaining oil. When hot, fry the garlic and chillies until brown. Reduce the heat and add the oyster sauce, soy sauce and palm sugar or honey; then gradually stir in the cornflour mixed with water. Spoon this sauce over the fried tofu and garnish with the crispy basil leaves. Serve immediately.

On our last night in Kuala Lumpur we were taken out to dinner in the revolving restaurant at the top of a tower that looks out over the whole city, with a spectacular view of the tallest building in the world, the Petronas towers. I made the classic mistake of putting my camera bag down on the floor next to the table. As the slowly rotating restaurant brought our table level with the Petronas towers I went to grab my camera, only to find that the whole bag had disappeared. After a moment of panic I realized that it was exactly where I had left it while we had travelled to the other side of the restaurant.

Tofu with Crispy Fried Basil and Chilli Sauce

HERB AND NOODLE SALAD

For this salad, mung bean noodles, available from Asian food stores, are dressed with a sweet and sour sauce and mixed with lots of fresh herbs. It can be served on its own or as a side dish. Don't bother to deep fry the tofu yourself — you can buy it.

6oz/175g deep-fried tofu, cut into ¼in/½cm slices

3oz/90g dried mung bean vermicelli noodles

6oz/175g wing beans or flat green beans, diagonally sliced and blanched for 1 minute

½ cucumber, cut into matchsticks

3 celery stalks, cut into matchsticks

5 spring onions, diagonally sliced

large handful of Thai sweet basil leaves, or basil

large handful of chopped mint leaves

8 tablespoons lime juice

3 tablespoons light soy sauce

3 red chillies, finely chopped

2 garlic cloves, crushed

2 tablespoons chopped palm sugar or honey

4 Chinese leaves, thinly sliced

For the garnish

5oz/150g bean sprouts

2 heaped tablespoons peanuts, finely chopped

1 tablespoon sesame seeds, dry roasted until brown

handful of chopped coriander leaves

Toast the tofu in an oil-free frying pan until brown on each side and set to one side.

Place the noodles in a bowl of boiling water for 10 minutes, and as they become pliable spread them out and cut into thirds with a pair of cooking scissors. Drain in a colander and rinse with cold water, place in a bowl and combine with the blanched wing beans or flat green beans, cucumber, celery, spring onions, basil and mint. In a separate bowl, mix the lime juice, soy sauce, chillies, garlic and palm sugar or honey until dissolved, pour over the noodles and mix well.

Serve individually on a bed of sliced Chinese leaves, topped with the noodles and garnished with the bean sprouts, chopped peanuts, sesame seeds, coriander and tofu slices.

MALACCAN LAKSA

For the garnish
1lb 5oz/600g fresh laksa rice noodles
    or 10oz/300g dried thick
    rice vermicelli
12oz/350g deep-fried tofu,
    cut into ½in/1cm slices
½ cucumber, cut into matchsticks
9oz/250g bean sprouts
large handful of chopped
    coriander leaves
large handful of roughly chopped
    Asian mint leaves
6 spring onions, finely sliced

For the paste
2 tablespoons coriander seeds
1 level teaspoon ground turmeric
4 red chillies, roughly chopped
3 stalks of lemon grass, thinly sliced
thumb-sized piece of galangal,
    peeled and thinly sliced
2 garlic cloves
15 small shallots, peeled
5 candlenuts or 10 skinless almonds
2 tablespoons dark soy sauce

For the soup
3 tablespoons sunflower oil
28fl oz/800ml coconut milk
8fl oz/250ml water
8oz/225g sugar snap peas
7oz/200g fine green beans, cut in half
salt to taste

To prepare the garnish ingredients, first cook the laksa noodles. If you are using fresh noodles, plunge them in boiling water for a few minutes and then drain. If you are using dried, boil a saucepan of water and add the noodles, cook for 5 minutes until the noodles are soft, drain and rinse with cold water, and place in a bowl. Put the remaining garnish ingredients in bowls and place on the table.

Next make the paste. Dry roast the coriander seeds in a small frying pan until aromatic, remove from the pan and grind to powder. Combine with all the remaining paste ingredients and grind to a paste in a food processor.

Now make the soup. Heat the oil in a wok. When hot, stir in the paste mix and fry for a few minutes. Add the coconut milk and water, bring to the boil and then reduce the heat and gently simmer for 5 minutes. Add the sugar snap peas, fine green beans and salt to taste, and cook for a couple of minutes.

Take the wok to the table. Put some of the noodles into your bowl, add the garnish ingredients you like the look of, and then ladle the soup over them.

Laksa is a meal in a bowl. It is bought from street stalls and eaten as a mid-morning snack, and it is also a very sociable meal to serve for friends: the garnish ingredients are placed in the middle of the table so that people can help themselves and the thick spicy coconut soup is poured over the top. *Laksa* noodles are made of rice and look like thick spaghetti. They are available from Asian food stores; however, you could substitute them with thick rice vermicelli.

Malaccan Laksa

STIR-FRIED VEGETABLES WITH GREEN PEPPERCORNS AND SHITAKE MUSHROOMS

Green peppercorns are young peppercorns; they are sold on their stems and available from good supermarkets or Asian stores. We use dried shitake mushrooms; however, you can use fresh instead if it's easier – just double the quantity.

4 tablespoons sunflower oil

3 large red chillies, sliced diagonally

6 spring onions, sliced diagonally

10 strings green peppercorns, broken in half

4oz/115g dried shitake mushrooms, soaked in hot water for 30 minutes and then sliced

9oz/250g fine green beans, cut in half

9oz/250g baby sweet corn, sliced lengthways

12oz/350g cauliflower florets

3 tablespoons dark soy sauce

1 tablespoon chopped palm sugar or honey

14fl oz/425ml vegetable stock

2 large handfuls of Thai sweet basil leaves, or basil

salt to taste

coriander leaves, to garnish

For the spice paste

4 dried red chillies, soaked in water until soft

4 garlic cloves, chopped

1 lemon grass stalk, sliced

3 shallots, sliced

4 coriander roots, chopped

1 teaspoon grated kaffir lime zest

½in/1cm galangal, grated

½ teaspoon coarsely ground black peppercorns

Blend the ingredients for the spice paste in a food processor until smooth.

Heat the oil in a wok. When hot, add the spice paste and sauté for a couple of minutes; then add the sliced large red chillies, spring onions and green peppercorns, stir into the paste and fry for 3 minutes. Add the mushrooms, green beans, baby sweet corn and cauliflower, and fry, stirring constantly until the vegetables start to soften. Then add the soy sauce, palm sugar or honey and vegetable stock. Cover the wok and simmer until the vegetables are just soft.

Add the basil and salt to taste, and serve with rice and Tofu with Crispy Fried Basil and Chilli Sauce (page 98).

Stir-fried Vegetables with Green Peppercorns and Shitake Mushrooms

CHU CHEE RED CURRY

Pad Thai (page 105) is a good accompaniment to this creamy red curry.

For the red curry paste
1 dessertspoon coriander seeds, dry
    roasted until aromatic and ground
5 dried red chillies, soaked in hot
    water until soft
3½ garlic cloves, chopped
1 lemon grass stalk, sliced
1 tablespoon chopped kaffir lime peel
4 coriander roots
1 tablespoon chopped galangal
5 shallots, chopped
2 tablespoons sunflower oil
2 garlic cloves, thinly sliced
16fl oz/500ml coconut milk
8fl oz/250ml vegetable stock

7oz/200g baby aubergines, cut into
    quarters, lengthways
7oz/200g mooli (white radishes), cut
    into thick matchsticks
4oz/115g button mushrooms
3½oz/100g oyster mushrooms, sliced
4oz/115g deep-fried tofu, cut into
    ¼in/½cm slices
2 tablespoons dark soy sauce
juice of ½ a kaffir lime or lime
1 tablespoon chopped palm sugar
    or honey
6 kaffir lime leaves, thinly sliced
salt to taste
2 large red chillies, thinly sliced,
    to garnish

Blend all the curry paste ingredients in a food processor until smooth.

Heat the oil in a wok. When hot, add the garlic and fry until brown, reduce the heat a little and stir in the curry paste; then add the coconut milk and vegetable stock. Add the vegetables, tofu, soy sauce, lime juice, palm sugar or honey and half the sliced lime leaves, and bring to the boil. Cover the pan, reduce the heat and gently simmer until the vegetables are cooked.

Add salt to taste and serve garnished with the remaining sliced lime leaves and the sliced large red chillies.

Above **The food market in Chaing Mai**

Right **A rice farmer with a buffalo at Dhara Dhevi, Chaing Mai**

PAD THAI

This is a one-dish meal that you can buy in street stalls all over Thailand. It's great for a quick lunch or as a side dish for a larger meal.

4 tablespoons sunflower oil

8 shallots, thinly sliced

4 garlic cloves, finely chopped

3 red chillies, thinly sliced

4 eggs, beaten

6oz/175g deep-fried tofu cut into ⅓in/1cm cubes

8oz/225g dried flat rice noodles

½ teaspoon chilli powder

½ teaspoon ground white pepper

4 tablespoons dark soy sauce

1 teaspoon tamarind paste, dissolved in 3 tablespoons of water

3 tablespoons lime juice

1 heaped tablespoon brown sugar

8 spring onions, sliced diagonally

10 tablespoons peanuts, dry roasted until brown and then ground until fine

12oz/350g bean sprouts

large handful of chopped coriander leaves, to garnish

Soften the rice noodles according to the directions on the packet. Heat the oil in a wok. When hot, add the sliced shallots, garlic and chillies, and fry until brown. Add the eggs, cook for a moment and then stir well. Add the tofu and fry for a minute or so. Add the softened noodles along with the chilli powder, white pepper, soy sauce, tamarind water, lime juice and brown sugar. Finally add half the spring onions, peanuts and bean sprouts. Place the rest of the spring onions, peanuts and bean sprouts on the table in bowls, along with the chopped coriander leaves to garnish and Sweet and Sour Dipping Sauce (page 106).

TEMPEH AND SHITAKE RICE PAPER ROLLS

2 tablespoons sunflower oil

2 garlic cloves, thinly sliced

2in/5cm piece of ginger, peeled and
   cut into thin strips

3 large mild red chillies, cut into long
   thin strips

1 teaspoon chopped coriander root

½ teaspoon coarsely ground black
   peppercorns

2oz/60g dried shitake mushrooms,
   soaked in boiling water for ½ hour
   and then sliced

3oz/90g tempeh, cut into large
   matchsticks

4 kaffir lime leaves, cut into thin
   strips

4 spring onions, shredded

small handful of chopped mint leaves

handful of bean sprouts

2 tablespoons lime juice

2 tablespoons light soy sauce

12 rice paper wrappers

Heat the oil in a wok. When hot, add the garlic, ginger, chillies, coriander root
and black peppercorns, and fry until brown. Add the sliced shitake mushrooms,
tempeh and lime leaves, and fry until the tempeh is crunchy and the mushrooms
are browned. Turn out into a bowl and allow to cool; then stir in the spring
onions, mint leaves, bean sprouts, lime juice and soy sauce.

Soak a rice paper wrapper in a bowl of hot water until soft, remove and dry
with kitchen paper. Place a twelfth of the filling down the centre, fold one end
over and roll. Repeat until you have used up all the sheets.

Serve with Sweet and Sour Dipping Sauce (below).

SWEET AND SOUR DIPPING SAUCE

6 tablespoons rice wine vinegar

4 tablespoons brown sugar

1 tablespoon lime juice

1 red chilli, finely chopped

1 green chilli, finely chopped

salt to taste

Gently heat the rice wine vinegar and sugar until the sugar is dissolved, and allow
to cool. Stir in the remaining ingredients.

Rice paper wrappers,
available dried from
Asian stores, are used to
roll the tempeh and
shitake mushroom
filling. The rolls are
then served with a
spicy sweet and sour
dipping sauce.

Right Tempeh
and Shitake Rice
Paper Rolls

Below Ingredients for
Tempeh and Shitake
Rice Paper Rolls

VEGETABLES IN A LEMON GRASS AND HERB-SCENTED BROTH

Fresh vegetables and dried mushrooms are combined in a tasty broth made with a curry paste packed with typical Thai flavours of lemon grass and galangal. The end result is a vegetarian version of an Oriental bisque.

For the curry paste
4 dried red chillies soaked in water
    until soft and then drained
2 lemon grass stalks, finely sliced
1 tablespoon finely chopped galangal
1 tablespoon chopped garlic
1½ oz/40g shallots, sliced
1 tablespoon ground turmeric

For the broth
2 pints/1.25 litres vegetable stock
½ oz/15g dried black fungus
    mushrooms or cloud ears, soaked
    in boiling water for 15 minutes
6oz/175g baby sweet corn,
    sliced lengthways

4oz/115g thin asparagus, cut into
    2in/5cm lengths
8oz/225g pak choi, cut into ¼in/1cm
    slices lengthways
8oz/225g bean sprouts
2 teaspoons chopped palm sugar
    or honey
3 tablespoons dark soy sauce
2 tablespoons lime juice
6 kaffir lime leaves, finely sliced
large handful of Thai sweet basil
    leaves, or basil
large handful of chopped
    coriander leaves
salt to taste

Make the curry paste by blending the ingredients in a food processor until smooth.

Heat the vegetable stock in a pan, and add the curry paste, drained black fungus, baby sweet corn and asparagus. Cover the pan and simmer until the vegetables are *al dente*. Add the pak choi, bean sprouts, palm sugar or honey, soy sauce, lime juice, lime leaves, basil and coriander leaves, simmer for a further minute and add salt to taste. Serve immediately.

CRISP VEGETABLE AND COCONUT SALAD

For this dish, fresh coconut is toasted and mixed with a crunchy salad. If you cannot get a fresh coconut, you can use desiccated coconut instead.

½ a small fresh coconut, finely grated, or 4 heaped tablespoons desiccated coconut

7oz/200g bean sprouts

½ medium cucumber, cut into matchsticks

7oz/200g sugar snap peas, sliced diagonally

5 spring onions, finely sliced

handful of chopped coriander leaves

handful of finely chopped Asian mint leaves

4 red chillies, finely chopped

For the dressing

3 tablespoons lime juice

3 tablespoons light soy sauce

1 dessertspoon honey

Toast the finely grated coconut or dessicated coconut in a small frying pan until golden, set to one side and allow to cool.

Combine the bean sprouts, cucumber, sugar snap peas, spring onions, coconut, coriander, mint and red chillies in a bowl. Mix the dressing ingredients, pour over the salad and mix well.

Allow the flavours to combine for 15 minutes before serving.

SAMBAL SAUCE

Sambal, a spicy sauce, usually accompanies every meal in Malaysia.

2 red chillies, finely chopped

1 tablespoon dark soy sauce

1 teaspoon tamarind paste

1 tablespoon lime juice

2 teaspoons honey

4 shallots, finely chopped

1 tomato, finely chopped

Blend all the ingredients in a food processor until finely chopped but not too smooth.

The Petronas towers of Kuala Lumpur at night

Islands of the

Indian Ocean

Islands of the Indian Ocean

Many of the islands of the Indian Ocean are the perfect image of a tropical paradise, with white sand beaches lapped by azure seas and fringed with lush coconut palms. Predictably, coconut milk and fresh fish are common ingredients in the islands' recipes. We have created vegetarian versions of some of the traditional fish dishes, being careful to keep the flavours that make them so delicious, and we found plenty more good and varied vegetarian dishes among the islands.

The ultimate paradise islands are the Maldives, tiny sand-bar atolls scattered among coral reefs in shallow lagoons of crystal-clear water. As far as local cuisine is concerned, it can be rather limited. Beyond the capital, Male, the few islands populated by Maldivians are little more than simple fishing villages, where people make do with what they can grow and catch. By contrast the islands occupied by resort hotels can afford to import ingredients to feed their guests. As the logistics of this are still complicated, chefs have to be inventive and devise their recipes with ingredients that can be stored easily for long periods and combine them with locally available ingredients to create exciting versions of traditional dishes.

Sri Lanka, the nearest Indian Ocean island to the Maldives, is large enough to have its own very distinctive cuisine. In our last book we included many recipes we found along the west coast and up in the hill country of the interior. Since then we have travelled to Trincomalee on the east coast where there is more of a Tamil influence in the dishes.

As it is the largest natural harbour in Asia and an historic port, we expected Trincomalee to be a thriving urban hub of industry and commerce. It is more like a laid-back seaside town out of season. The main street, a parade of single-storey shops, opens out on to a large park with a cricket stadium in the middle and sandy bays either side. Spotted deer wander about on the grass without a care in the world; worshippers drift in and out of the Hindu temple on one side, while fishermen mend their nets on the other. The busiest place in town is the Siva temple perched on Swami Rock high above the old Portuguese fort guarding the entrance to the harbour.

Home-cooked food on the islands of the Seychelles reflects the mix of Asian, African and European people who have settled on them over the years. Typical Creole cuisine is made with the ingredients that grow easily in people's gardens. There is hardly a home without breadfruit and apple trees, a vegetable patch and a herb garden. Pineapples, bananas and wild herbs grow in the forest and coconut palms are everywhere.

Pages 110–111 **A rock on the shore of La Digue island in the Seychelles**

Right, clockwise from top right **A typical white sand beach in the Maldives; children in a Maldivian fishing village; a spa pavilion at Taj Exotica; a traditional** *dhoni* **fishing boat in Male harbour; the Indian Ocean**

CORIANDER CHEELA

Cheela is a savoury gluten-free pancake made from gram flour (chickpea flour) Easy to make, it's a perfect quick meal. We have it for supper, stuffed with mung bean sprouts fried for 1 minute and sprinkled with lemon juice. It is also a brilliant alternative to rice and works well with Maldivian Mango and Chickpea Curry (page 117).

MAKES 12 PANCAKES

12oz / 350g gram flour	2 teaspoons baking powder
2 tablespoons cumin seeds, dry roasted until aromatic	1 teaspoon salt
	1 pint / 500ml water
1 tablespoon coriander seeds, dry roasted until aromatic and crushed	2 medium eggs, whisked
	1 large red onion, finely chopped
1 dessertspoon black peppercorns, crushed	large handful of chopped coriander leaves

Sieve the flour into a bowl, and stir in the spices, baking powder and salt. Gradually whisk in the water and eggs until a batter forms. Set to one side for half an hour.

Stir in the chopped red onion and coriander leaves. Heat a little oil in a non-stick pan. When hot, pour 3¼ fl oz / 100ml of batter into the pan, reduce the heat a little and cook until brown. Carefully turn and cook the other side. Serve immediately.

PAPAYA CHUTNEY

This works really well with Paneer Tikka (page 118) and Spicy Rice Flat Bread (page 119).

2 tablespoons sunflower oil	4 spring onions, finely sliced
2 teaspoons black mustard seeds	2 large tomatoes, cubed
½ teaspoon ground turmeric	1in / 2.5cm piece of ginger, grated
½ teaspoon ground black pepper	2 tablespoons lime juice
2 small papayas, peeled, deseeded and cubed	salt to taste

Heat the oil in a frying pan. When hot, add the mustard seeds and when they crackle add the turmeric, black pepper and papaya. Fry for a couple of minutes and then turn out into a bowl. Add the spring onions, tomatoes, grated ginger, lime juice and salt to taste.

No meal in the islands is complete without a selection of salads – such as sweet apples grated with ginger and then tossed with Chinese leaf and lemon juice – and *chatinis* (chutneys). Papaya is not only used in chutney but also blended with garlic and thyme into a soup, which is served with thin chips of fried breadfruit.

Evening fishing in a bay on Mahé Island in the Seychelles

DATE AND TAMARIND CHUTNEY

2 dessertspoons tamarind paste,
   dissolved in 12fl oz/350ml water
9oz/250g dates, stoned and
   finely chopped
2 garlic cloves, finely chopped
thumb-sized piece of ginger,
   peeled and grated

1 teaspoon chilli powder
2 tablespoons honey
juice of 2 limes
2in/5cm piece of cinnamon
1 teaspoon salt
2oz/60g sultanas
25 cashew nuts, roughly chopped

Combine all the ingredients except the cashews in a saucepan and bring to the boil. Cover the pan and gently simmer until the dates have cooked down and are of chutney consistency. Finally add the cashew nuts and cook for a further 5 minutes. Allow to cool. Pour into a jar and store in the fridge until required.

MALDIVIAN MANGO AND CHICKPEA CURRY

4 tablespoons butter

1 large red onion, finely chopped

3 garlic cloves, finely chopped

1in/2.5cm piece of ginger, peeled and grated

10 curry leaves

1 dessertspoon black mustard seeds

1 teaspoon ground coriander

½ teaspoon ground cinnamon

½ teaspoon ground cardamom

½ teaspoon ground turmeric

½ teaspoon ground black pepper

1lb/450g butternut squash, peeled and cubed

2 large tomatoes, chopped

1 cup water

14oz/400g cooked chickpeas

2 large mangoes, peeled and cubed

8fl oz/250ml coconut milk

4fl oz/125ml yoghurt

1 tablespoon lime juice

salt to taste

Melt the butter in a wok, add the onion, garlic, ginger and curry leaves, and sauté until the onion is soft. Add the mustard seeds, and when they crackle, add the remaining spices, stirring them into the butter. Add the cubed butternut squash and the tomatoes, and sauté until the squash starts to soften. Add the water and the chickpeas, bring to the boil, cover the pan and simmer for 5 minutes. Add the chopped mangoes and coconut milk, cover the pan and gently simmer for 10 minutes. Stir in the yoghurt, lime juice and salt to taste. Serve with Coriander Cheela (page 114) or rice.

FRESH COCONUT WITH LIME

A good accompaniment to any curry.

½ a fresh coconut

1 garlic clove, finely chopped

2 green chillies, finely chopped

juice of 2 limes

salt to taste

Place the coconut in a plastic bag and give it a good bash with a rolling pin. Remove the flesh from the shell. Cut the coconut into strips with a vegetable peeler. Combine the remaining ingredients and pour over the coconut strips. Allow to marinate for 1 hour or so before serving.

Coriander Cheela (page 114) with Maldivian Mango and Chickpea Curry

PANEER TIKKA

1lb 2oz/500g paneer, cut into 1in/2.5cm cubes	1 teaspoon cumin seeds
4 garlic cloves	½ cinnamon stick
2 in/5cm piece of ginger, peeled and grated	1 teaspoon black peppercorns
1 teaspoon salt	3 bay leaves
juice of 2 lemons	1 teaspoon ground cardamon
1 tablespoon coriander seeds	2 teaspoons ground turmeric
1 teaspoon cloves	½ pint/300ml Greek-style yoghurt
1 teaspoon whole mace	3 tablespoons sunflower oil
	salt to taste

Skewer the paneer cubes on to 12 small skewers. Blend the garlic, ginger, salt and lemon juice until a paste forms, coat the paneer cubes with the paste and set to one side.

Dry roast the whole spices and bay leaves in a small frying pan until aromatic, remove from the pan and grind to a powder; then add the ground spices. Whisk the yoghurt and oil together in a bowl, and stir in the spice mix. Season to taste and coat the paneer skewers with the spiced yoghurt. Leave to marinate for 1 hour. Cook the skewers under the grill, in a griddle pan or on the barbeque until brown on all sides. Baste with a little of the marinade. Serve immediately. Papaya Chutney (page 114) and Spicy Rice Flat Bread (opposite) are the perfect accompaniments.

BRINJAL PICKLE

This is a very quick and easy-to-make pickle that can be served immediately.

1 small aubergine, thinly sliced	2 green chillies, finely chopped
salt and ground turmeric to season the aubergine	1 dessertspoon yellow mustard seeds, ground
sunflower oil	juice of 2 limes
1 medium red onion, thinly sliced	1 teaspoon honey

Season the aubergine slices with a little salt and turmeric; then heat the oil in a frying pan and fry until soft. Place in a bowl. Combine the remaining ingredients and pour over the aubergine. Allow to stand for 30 minutes before serving.

Twenty years ago I boarded an overcrowded, rusting ferry for the short sea voyage between India and Sri Lanka. Several hours after our scheduled departure, there was an announcement in Tamil which instantly caused a frenzied flight from the deck. Fearful that the ferry might be about to sink, I joined the fight for the exit. With relief I found that those in the exodus were merely heading for the ship's restaurant for a free meal that had been offered as compensation for the delay. My dining companions were unanimous in recommending Sri Lanka's east coast around the port of Trincomalee as the perfect beach to head for after visiting the island's hill stations and ancient cities.

I never made it to Trincomalee. Soon afterwards, simmering disputes between the Sinhalese Buddhists and Tamil Hindus erupted into violent conflict. Until recently civil war between the Sri Lankan military and the Liberation

SPICY RICE FLAT BREAD

You can eat this gluten-free bread spread with a little butter as a snack or with a meal instead of rice. It can be kept in the fridge for a day or so if you want to make it in advance.

14oz/400g rice flour	1 dessertspoon ground turmeric
1 teaspoon salt	5 garlic cloves
2 tablespoons sunflower oil	2in/5cm piece of ginger,
1 medium red onion, finely chopped	peeled and grated
1–2 teaspoons red chilli flakes	butter, to serve

Place the rice flour in a saucepan and gently roast for a few minutes without browning. Add the salt and gradually stir in boiling water until a dough forms. Set to one side and allow to cool to room temperature.

Meanwhile heat the oil in a frying pan. When hot, add the red onion and fry until soft. Add the spices, fry for 1 minute and mix thoroughly with the dough. Allow to rest for 10 minutes.

Roll out a golfball-sized piece of dough, dusted with rice flour, until flat. Smear a little oil in a non-stick frying pan and cook the bread on both sides until brown. Repeat until you have used all the dough. Serve spread with a little butter.

SRI LANKAN ROASTED CURRY POWDER

This spice mix is typical of Sri Lanka. It is not tempered but added at the end like a garam masala. We always make it in advance and store in an airtight container.

1 tablespoon white rice	1 teaspoon cloves
1 tablespoon coriander seeds	20 curry leaves
1 dessertspoon cumin seeds	1 teaspoon black peppercorns
1 tablespoon desiccated coconut	1 teaspoon black mustard seeds
2in/5cm piece of cinnamon	

Dry roast the rice in a small frying pan until it starts to brown. Add all the spices and dry roast until they become aromatic and the coconut is golden brown. Remove from the heat and grind to a powder.

CASHEW NUT STUFFED CAPSICUM IN A COCONUT AND CURRY LEAF SAUCE

Sweet capsicums look like large chillies but they are not spicy. They are available in both green and red varieties. We prefer red, but if you can only find green that's fine. They vary in size, so when choosing take into account how many you can eat.

10–12 sweet capsicums	½ teaspoon chilli powder
1 large red onion, roughly chopped	1 tablespoon water
1 tablespoon fish sauce or soy sauce (optional)	3 tablespoons sunflower oil
	2 green chillies, finely chopped
1 tablespoon lime juice	½ teaspoon ground turmeric
2 tablespoons desiccated coconut	20 curry leaves
4oz/115g cashew nuts	14fl oz/400ml coconut milk
2 teaspoons roasted curry powder (page 119)	salt to taste

Wash the capsicums and then slit each one down one side and carefully remove the seeds, without breaking the capsicum.

Make the filling by blending together the chopped red onion, fish or soy sauce, lime juice, desiccated coconut, cashew nuts, 1 teaspoon of the roasted curry powder, the chilli powder and the water until a paste forms. Stuff the capsicums with the filling and then heat the oil in a heavy frying pan and fry them on each side for a few minutes until brown. Remove from the pan and set to one side.

Add the chopped green chillies, turmeric and curry leaves to the pan, fry for a couple of minutes, and then reduce the heat and add the coconut milk, salt to taste and stuffed capsicums. Bring to the boil and gently simmer until the capsicums are soft and the sauce has reduced. Finally sprinkle the rest of the roasted curry powder over the top, cover the pan and allow to sit for 2 minutes before serving with rice.

Cashew Nut Stuffed Capsicum in a Coconut and Curry Leaf Sauce

It was well worth being up at dawn for a swim in the warm, clear sea, and then a walk along the shore before breakfast. Fishing boats that spend all night at sea, their lamps twinkling on the horizon like the stars filling the sky, return in the morning to unload their booty. Rows of men haul immense nets ashore, and traders gather to barter for their share of the catch. Breakfast was always worth the wait; it was here that we discovered the pleasure of an omelette curry.

A *dhoni* fishing boat setting out to sea in the Maldives

OMELETTE CURRY

For the omelette
5 large free-range eggs
2 medium red onions, diced
3 green chillies, finely chopped
10 curry leaves
large handful of chopped
    coriander leaves
juice of ½ a lime
1 dessertspoon fish sauce or soy sauce
    (optional)
sunflower oil, to fry

For the gravy
2 tablespoons sunflower oil
2 medium red onions, finely sliced
2 green chillies, finely chopped
15 curry leaves
2 teaspoons cumin seeds
1 teaspoon turmeric
14fl oz/400ml coconut milk
1 dessertspoon fish sauce or soy sauce
    (optional)
juice of 1 lime
1 heaped teaspoon roasted curry
    powder (page 119)
salt to taste

First make three omelettes. Whisk the eggs in a bowl and then stir in the remaining ingredients. Divide the mixture into three. Heat a little sunflower oil in a frying pan and when hot, pour in a third of the mixture. When one side is cooked, carefully turn and cook the other side. Cut the omelette into quarters and set to one side. Repeat until you have three omelettes.

To make the gravy, heat 2 tablespoons of sunflower oil in a wok. When hot, add the sliced onions and gently sauté until soft. Stir in the chillies and spices, fry for 1 minute, and add the coconut milk and fish or soy sauce. Gently simmer for 10 minutes, taking care not to boil, as the coconut milk will split. Add the lime juice, salt to taste and omelette quarters, and simmer for a few minutes. Finally sprinkle the roasted curry powder over the top, cover the pan, turn off the heat and allow to sit for a few minutes.

Serve with rice and Date and Tamarind Chutney (page 115).

DEVILLED POTATO CURRY

This simple curry is delicious with Coconut Mellun Chutney (below) and Bringal Pickle (page 118).

4 tablespoons sunflower oil

1 large red onion, finely sliced

3 green chillies, finely chopped

½ teaspoon chilli powder

20 curry leaves

2 teaspoons dill seeds

2 teaspoons black mustard seeds

1½lb/750g potatoes, peeled and
  boiled until soft, and then cut
  into cubes

1 tablespoon fish sauce or soy sauce
  (optional)

6fl oz/190ml water

salt to taste

Heat the oil in a wok. When hot, add the onion and fry until soft. Add the chillies, chilli powder, curry leaves, dill seeds and mustard seeds, and fry for 1 minute. Add the cooked potatoes, fish or soy sauce and water, and gently simmer until the water has reduced and the potatoes start to brown, stirring to avoid sticking. Add salt to taste.

COCONUT MELLUN CHUTNEY

1 tablespoon sunflower oil

1 medium onion, finely chopped

2 green chillies, finely chopped

¼ teaspoon ground turmeric

20 curry leaves

3oz/90g desiccated coconut

4fl oz/125ml water

juice of 1 lime

salt to taste

Heat the oil in a saucepan. When hot, add the onion and chillies, and sauté until the onion is soft. Stir in the turmeric and curry leaves, and fry for 1 minute. Add the coconut and water, and gently simmer until the water is absorbed. Add the lime juice and season to taste.

*Pages 124–125,
clockwise from top right*
A Hindu temple on Trincomalee beach, Sri Lanka; fishermen at Trincomalee; La Digue island in the Seychelles; the Buddhas of Polonnaruwa, Sri Lanka; a fishing boat lamp; a Hindu temple in Trincomalee

THYME AND LEMON RICE

A perfect accompaniment to Seychelloise food.

2 tablespoons butter
grated zest of 2 lemons
1 tablespoon chopped fresh thyme
½ teaspoon freshly ground
    black pepper

1lb/450g basmati rice, washed until
    the water runs clear
juice of 1 lemon
salt to taste

Melt the butter in a medium saucepan, add the lemon, thyme and black pepper, and sauté for 1 minute. Add the washed rice and stir until the rice is coated with the butter; then add the lemon juice and enough cold water to cover the rice by ½in/1cm. Cover the pan and bring to the boil, reduce the heat, and gently cook until all the water is absorbed. Season to taste.

BANANA AND CHILLI FRITTER WITH PASSION FRUIT DIP

For the passion fruit dip
½ teaspoon mustard
juice of 1 lime
4 tablespoons olive oil
6 passion fruit, cut in half and the
    flesh scooped out
salt and freshly ground pepper to taste

For the fritters
4 tablespoons butter
2 eggs, lightly beaten
16fl oz/500ml natural yoghurt
2 teaspoons honey
8oz/225g plain flour

½ teaspoon salt
1 tablespoon baking powder
2 red chillies, finely chopped
3 large ripe bananas, mashed with
    a fork
sunflower oil

For the garnish
1 Chinese leaf, thinly sliced
sunflower oil
2in/5cm piece of ginger,
    peeled and grated
salt and freshly ground black pepper
    to taste

First make the passion fruit dip. Mix the mustard and lime juice in a bowl, and then gradually stir in the oil. Stir in the passion fruit and season to taste.

Melt the butter and allow to cool to room temperature. Mix the eggs, yoghurt and honey, and combine with the flour, salt and baking powder. Finally stir in the chillies and mashed banana. Heat a little sunflower oil in a non-stick frying pan. When hot, spoon the mixture into the pan in round fritter shapes and cook until bubbles form; then turn and cook the other sides.

Serve immediately, drizzled with the passion fruit dressing and garnished with thinly sliced Chinese leaf fried in a little sunflower oil. Add the grated ginger and season with salt and freshly ground black pepper to taste.

GREEN MANGO PICKLE

It seems that most mangoes we buy in supermarkets are underripe, which is useful for this recipe as it means that you can use them straight away without having to wait for them to ripen.

Left Bananas

Below Women on their way home from the shop on La Digue island in the Seychelles

2 underripe mangoes
1 red chilli, finely chopped
1in/2.5cm piece of ginger, peeled
 and grated
2 garlic cloves, finely chopped
1 stick of lemon grass, finely sliced

1 teaspoon fish sauce or soy sauce
 (optional)
juice of 2 limes
handful of chopped coriander leaves
1 teaspoon honey
salt and pepper to taste

Combine all the ingredients and then chill in the fridge for 30 minutes before serving.

CINNAMON AND COCONUT MILK CURRY

3 tablespoons sunflower oil

1 large red onion, thinly sliced

2 garlic cloves, finely chopped

1½in/4cm piece of ginger, peeled and grated

2 green chillies, finely chopped

14oz/400g peeled and cubed butternut squash

1 cinnamon stick, broken into 1in/2.5cm pieces

6oz/175g green beans, topped and tailed

4 celery sticks, cut into diagonal ½in/1cm slices

3 medium courgettes, cut into diagonal ½in/1cm slices

8fl oz/250ml water

⅔ small head of Chinese leaves, cut into 1in/2.5cm strip

2 sticks of lemon grass, finely sliced

handful of chopped parsley

1 tablespoon chopped thyme leaves

14fl oz/400ml coconut milk

salt to taste

For the curry powder

1 teaspoon ground cumin

1 teaspoon ground coriander

½ teaspoon ground cardamon

1 teaspoon ground turmeric

½ teaspoon ground fennel

1 teaspoon chilli powder

½ teaspoon ground cloves

½ teaspoon ground black pepper

15 curry leaves

Combine all the curry powder ingredients.

Heat the oil in a wok. When hot, add the onion, garlic, ginger and chillies, and sauté until the onion is soft. Add the butternut squash and cook until it starts to soften; then add the spice mix and the broken cinnamon stick, and cook for 1 minute. Add the green beans, celery, courgettes and water, and bring to the boil. Cover the wok, reduce the heat and gently simmer for 5 minutes. Add the Chinese leaves, lemon grass, parsley, thyme and coconut milk, cover the wok again and gently simmer for a further 10 minutes or so until the vegetables are soft and the sauce has reduced.

Season to taste and serve with Thyme and Lemon Rice (page 127).

Elephants bathing in the river at Pinnewala, Sri Lanka

MARINATED HALLOUMI WITH SEYCHELLOISE ROUGAILLE SAUCE

This dish is traditionally made with fish but halloumi is a good substitute. Blimbi are small cucumber-shaped vegetables that grow in most Seychelloise gardens; gherkins are similar, so we use them instead.

1lb 2oz/500g halloumi, cut into
   ½/1cm strips

For the marinade
2 sticks of lemon grass, thinly sliced
1in/2.5cm piece of ginger, peeled
   and grated
2 garlic cloves, finely chopped
1 green chilli, finely chopped
½ teaspoon ground turmeric
grated zest of 1 lime
juice of 1 lime
1 tablespoon sunflower oil

For the rougaille sauce
3 tablespoons sunflower oil

1 large red onion, diced
4 cloves garlic, finely chopped
2in/5cm piece of ginger, peeled
   and grated
2 green chillies, finely chopped
1 dessertspoon black mustard seeds
½ teaspoon freshly ground
   black pepper
10oz/300g cherry tomatoes,
   chopped in a blender
1 tablespoon soy sauce
6 gherkins, diced
4 spring onions, sliced
1 tablespoon chopped thyme leaves
handful of chopped parsley leaves
salt to taste

Combine the marinade ingredients and pour over the halloumi slices. Leave to marinade for 1 hour. Cook the marinated halloumi on a barbeque, under the grill or on a griddle until brown on each side. Retain any of the marinade that is left.

Heat the oil in a saucepan. When hot, add the onion, garlic, ginger and chillies, and sauté until the onion is soft. Add the mustard seeds and black pepper and fry for 1 minute. Add the chopped cherry tomatoes, soy sauce, gherkins, spring onions, thyme, parsley and retained marinade, and bring to the boil; then reduce the heat, cover and gently simmer until the sauce reduces and the oil returns. Add salt to taste.

Serve the sauce on the side of the grilled halloumi with Creole Pumpkin Chutney (opposite).

Marinated Halloumi
with Seychelloise
Rougaille Sauce

CREOLE PUMPKIN CHUTNEY

1½lb/750g peeled and cubed
    butternut squash
1in/2.5cm piece of ginger, peeled
    and grated
2 garlic cloves, finely chopped
1 red chilli, finely chopped
1 dessertspoon chopped thyme leaves

small handful of chopped
    coriander leaves
½ teaspoon freshly ground black pepper
2 tablespoons olive oil
juice of ½ a lemon
1 teaspoon honey
4 spring onions, finely sliced
salt to taste

Stew the butternut squash in a covered saucepan with the ginger, garlic, chilli and a splash of water until soft. Mash the squash and then stir in the remaining ingredients.

Islands of French

Polynesia

As soon as we arrived, we had an overwhelming feeling that we were in a good place. Nuka Hiva, the largest of the French Polynesian Marquesas Islands, right out in the middle of the vastness of the Pacific Ocean, is one of the most hospitable, beautiful destinations we have visited. Hidden in the tropical vegetation and dramatic mountainous landscape are many ancient sites, such as Koueva, a vast clearing with ancient stone platforms, sacrificial altars and statues overgrown with creepers and vines. Tourism is still a novelty.

The drive to Taiohae was a wonderful introduction to the island. We climbed up a track through pine forests and ravines to a pass between jagged mountain peaks. Ahead mountains stretched like a massive amphitheatre around the Toovii plateau. Once across the plain, we descended through a landscape of towering round-topped hills in forested valleys reminiscent of a Chinese scroll painting. Then a great vista revealed a scattering of buildings around a bay of blue water dotted with yachts.

Taiohae is an easy-going town, spread out along the beach. Everyone knows each other and they soon get to know you. Traditional sculpture, carving and tattooing are still part of everyday life. Invitations to people's homes to see these activities come easily, blissfully free of any hard sell. Many of the men of Nuka Hiva have heavily tattooed muscular bodies yet avoid being intimidating by wearing flowers in their hair and offering broad smiles at every meeting. Many of the women share their good looks and confidence. It was the natural beauty of the Marquesas and their people that attracted Paul Gauguin to make his final home on neighbouring Hiva Oa.

We set off east over the mountains to the lush river valley of Taipivai, which leads up to a high pass, looking down on waterfalls cascading out of the forest on one side and the sandy bay of Hatiheu on the other. Inland from the north shore are two archaeological sites, larger and even more atmospheric than Koueva: Hikokua and Kamuihei, where there are extensive remains of temples, pyramid altars, platforms, tikis and pits used to fatten up sacrificial victims for cannibal feasts. In the past warring tribes practised cannibalism as a symbol of victory.

We had a much more palatable introduction to traditional cuisine at a beachside café. Chez Yvonne served us a Marquesan feast of coconut and sweet potato soup, then an *ahimaa* of breadfruits, sweet potatoes and plantains accompanied by various salads. We took a very necessary rest after this on the beautiful white sand beach at Anaho Bay. Like the food, we found that the beauty of Nuka Hiva is both more delicate and dramatic than the more obvious charms of Tahiti, Bora Bora and Rangiroa. It was well worth the extra effort needed to get there.

Pages 134–135 **Hatiheu Bay on Nuku Hiva, one of the Marquesas Islands**

Right, clockwise from top right **Leg tattoo on Nuku Hiva warrior; a tiki statue; a young would–be warrior at Taiohae; the church at Hatiheu; a Polynesian girl in Taipivai; the Tohua Koueva ruins of Pakoko's jungle capital on Nuku Hiva**

This dish takes its name from the Polynesian style of cooking food in an *ahimaa*. This is a hole dug in the ground and lined with kindling and stones. The kindling is lit and banana leaves are placed on top of the stones. Food is placed on the leaves – usually a suckling pig, fish or vegetables. The hole is then covered with leaves and sand and the food allowed to cook for several hours. Today this time-consuming method is frequently replaced by marinating ingredients and cooking them on a barbecue.

The marinade is a traditional one, using the tropical French spice mix *quatre épices*, a mixture of black pepper, nutmeg, ginger and clove. We think this works well with tempeh (fermented soya bean curd), which is available from health food or Asian stores; however, if you find it hard to buy, tofu or vegetables work as well.

Polynesian Maa Tahiti Tempeh with Sweet Peppers and Haricot Beans

POLYNESIAN MAA TAHITI TEMPEH

1lb/450g tempeh, cut into
 ½in/1cm slices

For the marinade
1 medium onion, chopped
2 garlic cloves, chopped
1 tablespoon olive oil
2 tablespoons thick coconut milk
grated zest of 1 lime
2 tablespoons lime juice

1 dessertspoon honey
1 teaspoon coarsely ground black
 peppercorns
½ teaspoon ground cloves
½ teaspoon grated nutmeg
1 teaspoon ground ginger
½ teaspoon cayenne pepper
salt to taste

Blend all the marinade ingredients until smooth and then coat the tempeh with the marinade and allow to stand for 1 hour. You can then cook the tempeh under the grill, on a griddle, in the oven or on a barbeque – take your pick.

Serve with Sweet Peppers and Haricot Beans (below), green salad and freshly baked baguette.

SWEET PEPPERS AND HARICOT BEANS

4 tablespoons butter
2 medium onions, cubed
3 garlic cloves, finely chopped
2 red peppers, sliced
1 teaspoon ground cinnamon
½ teaspoon cracked black peppercorns
½ teaspoon cayenne pepper

5 medium tomatoes, chopped
1lb/450g cooked haricot beans
4fl oz/125ml white wine
1 tablespoon chopped sage leaves
1 handful chopped parsley
salt to taste

Melt the butter in a thick-bottomed pan, add the onions, garlic and red peppers, and sauté until soft. Stir in the spices and cook for 1 minute. Add the chopped tomatoes, haricot beans, white wine and herbs, and bring to the boil; then cover the pan, reduce the heat and gently simmer until the sauce reduces and the oil returns.

Season to taste and serve with Polynesian Maa Tahiti Tempeh (above), green salad and freshly baked baguette.

COCONUT AND SWEET POTATO SOUP

3 tablespoons butter

2 medium onions, diced

2 garlic cloves, finely chopped

1½lb/750g sweet potato

½ teaspoon ground cinnamon

½ teaspoon coarsely ground
  black peppercorns

½ teaspoon grated nutmeg

½ teaspoon ground cloves

½–1 teaspoon cayenne pepper

1½ pints/750ml vegetable stock

½ pint/250ml coconut milk

salt to taste

handful of chopped coriander leaves,
  to garnish

Melt the butter in a saucepan, add the onions and garlic, and sauté until soft. Add the sweet potato and fry until it starts to soften. Stir in the spices and fry for 1 minute. Add the stock and bring to the boil; then reduce the heat, cover the pan and simmer until the sweet potato is soft. Add the coconut milk and simmer for 5 minutes or so. Blend the soup until smooth. Return it to the heat and gently heat until hot enough to serve, adding extra water if necessary.

Add salt to taste and serve garnished with chopped coriander leaves and warm baguette.

Above Taiohae Bay on Nuku Hiva; *right* Bora Bora lagoon in the Society Islands

POLYNESIAN SALAD WITH COCONUT MILK DRESSING

3 medium carrots, grated

2 red peppers, diced

3 medium tomatoes, diced

1 tablespoon sunflower oil

1 plantain, peeled and sliced into oval
 shapes ¾ in / 2 cm thick

1 medium red onion, diced

4 large free-range eggs, hard-boiled
 and then crushed

For the dressing

2 garlic cloves, crushed

juice of 2 limes

3½ fl oz / 115 ml coconut milk

1 teaspoon red wine vinegar

1 teaspoon coarsely ground
 black peppercorns

handful of parsley, finely chopped

Tabasco to taste

salt to taste

Combine the grated carrots, red peppers and tomatoes in a bowl.

To make the dressing, mix the garlic, lime juice, coconut milk, red wine vinegar, black pepper, parsley, Tabasco and salt to taste.

Heat the oil in a frying pan. When hot, fry the plantain until it begins to brown on the outside and soften. Pour the dressing over the salad and top with the fried plantain, red onion and crushed egg.

BAKED PAPAYA AND BANANA POE

We ate this dish, accompanied by Polynesian Salad with Coconut Milk Dressing (above), as a communal meal with all the other guests at a simple pension on Rangiroa Island on our way to Nuku Hiva. Together the two dishes make a good outdoor meal for a summer evening.

2 medium papayas, peeled, deseeded
 and cut into cubes

2 medium plantains, peeled
 and cubed

cayenne pepper, to taste

½ teaspoon coarsely ground
 black peppercorns

1 vanilla pod, split down the middle

salt to taste

4 fl oz / 125 ml coconut milk

Place all the ingredients except the coconut milk in baking foil and fold to make a sealed parcel. Bake in an oven, preheated to 400°F / 200°C, for 25 minutes or so, until soft. Remove from the oven, open the parcel and sprinkle the coconut milk over the top. Reseal and allow to sit for 10 minutes before serving.

Left The interior of
Nuku Hiva

Above A Tiki statue on
Hiva Oa

Central America

Central America

On this visit to Central America we went in search of recipes in Guatemala and Belize. As well as a huge choice of suitable local cuisine, both countries had plenty of other attractions to make them well worth a visit.

The faded charm of Antigua's sixteenth-century Spanish colonial architecture and its dramatic setting between three volcanic peaks make it one of the most beautiful cities in the Americas. The descendants of the Maya who live here have incorporated the religion of the conquistadors into their culture in some unique ways. The night we arrived people were gathered in the town's plazas and cobbled streets to burn giant effigies of the devil. Outside La Merced church a life-like doll of St Diego Juan was being paraded, while a cacophony of exploding fireworks echoed through the streets. The next morning a breakfast of refried beans, scrambled eggs, guacamole and other dishes – our first introduction to Guatemalan food – offered good hope for our quest.

In the colourful, chaotic city market, traders from mountain villages mingled with locals selling fabrics, food and fireworks. Guatemala is one of the world's few sources of jade, which can be found here at bargain prices. But we searched in vain for recipes.

We travelled north to Tikal to visit the great Mayan pyramid temples that tower above the canopy of Guatemala's northern jungle. Climbing to the top of the highest pyramid and looking down over the summits of the other temples poking out above the forest below, alive with the eerie screeching of howler monkeys and squawking of parrots, was unforgettable. The vegetarian options unfortunately were few.

We had more success in Mountain Pine Ridge, a short drive over the border into Belize. Here we found a great vegetable stew flavoured with *achiote*, a combination of allspice, cumin, cinnamon and annatto seeds. We joined an excursion to some local river caves, entering them in canoes and using lamps to see human skulls left in ancient Mayan burial sites. Sometimes we were in cathedral-sized chambers; at others we had to negotiate places where the cave roof was only inches above us. The next day, we canoed in fresh air and sunshine on the Macal river at Chaa creek, where giant iguanas lazed around on rocks along the bank, and then headed for the coast.

We found Placencia, perched on a narrow peninsula of white sand stretching out into the Caribbean, a laid-back, barefoot seaside town of brightly painted wooden houses on stilts. The local 'green and clean committee' sponsors signs along its narrow car-free main street which encourage people not to drop litter that might harm its shoeless residents. They are written in the Creole dialect of English spoken by the Afro-Caribbean people who dominate coastal Belize. Here we ate a very interesting and unusual version of cauliflower cheese.

Pages 142–143 **The ruins of the Mayan city of Tikal in the Guatemalan jungle**

Right, clockwise from top right **A doorway in Antigua, Guatemala; San Pedro island in Belize; a doorway in Guatemala; one of the Mayan pyramids on Tikal; a window in Antigua; a street in Antigua**

PLACENCIA COCONUT CAULIFLOWER WITH MELTED CHEESE

This unusual take on cauliflower cheese works surprisingly well. Coconut milk, ginger, cashew nuts, chillies and cheese are combined to make a uniquely Belizean dish.

2¼lb/1kg cauliflower florets
2 tablespoons chopped ginger
15fl oz/450ml coconut milk
salt and freshly ground black pepper
    to taste
4–6 green chillies, thinly sliced
2oz/60g cashew nuts, ground in a
    food processor or pestle and
    mortar to make a powder

10 shallots, peeled and cut in half
large handful of chopped
    coriander leaves
2oz/60g ghee or butter
6oz/175g grated strong hard cheese,
    such as mature cheddar or sheep's
    cheese if you are avoiding dairy

Place the cauliflower, ginger, coconut milk, and salt and pepper to taste in a large saucepan. Cover the pan and gently simmer until all the liquid has reduced – at this point the cauliflower should be half cooked. Stir in the chillies, ground cashew nuts, shallots, coriander and ghee or butter, cover with the grated cheese and bake in the oven, preheated to 400°F/200°C, for about 15 minutes or until the cheese is melted and nice and brown. Serve with new potatoes and salad.

In this recipe a spicy roux is made and then vegetables are added to make a traditional stew that is eaten in most homes. Annatto seeds are red seeds that give dishes a characteristic ochre colour. They are the principal ingredient of *achiote*, which is a combination of cinnamon, cumin and allspice. If you can't find them, use paprika instead and slightly reduce the amount of allspice, cinnamon and cumin.

Mayan pyramids rising out of the jungle at Tikal in Guatemala

MOUNTAIN PINE RIDGE STEW

12oz/350g new potatoes, cubed
2 red peppers, sliced
2 green peppers, sliced
4 tablespoons olive oil
1 red onion, thinly sliced
5 celery sticks, thinly sliced
3 garlic cloves, crushed
3 green chillies, thinly sliced
1 heaped teaspoon ground annatto
    seeds or paprika

1 teaspoon allspice
1 teaspoon ground cumin
½ teaspoon ground cinnamon
3 tablespoons chopped oregano leaves
3 tablespoons fine cornmeal
24fl oz/750ml vegetable water
2 large handfuls of baby spinach leaves
salt and freshly ground black pepper
    to taste
handful of chopped coriander leaves

Boil the potatoes and peppers until just soft, drain and retain the vegetable water, and set to one side.

Heat the olive oil in a large heavy-bottomed pan. When hot, add the onion, celery, garlic and chillies, and sauté until soft. Add the spices and oregano. Stir in the cornmeal, fry for a couple of minutes and then gradually add 3 cups of the retained vegetable water, stirring constantly until a sauce forms. Add the potatoes, peppers, spinach, salt and pepper to taste, and simmer for a further 5 minutes.

Serve garnished with chopped coriander leaves with Corn and Black Bean Salsa with Toasted Pumpkin Seeds (page 150), sour cream and flour tortillas.

CORN AND BLACK BEAN SALSA WITH TOASTED PUMPKIN SEEDS

9oz/250g sweet corn kernels, fresh, frozen or tinned

9oz/250g cooked black beans or kidney beans

1 large red pepper, diced

1 red onion, diced

1 jalapeño chilli or 2 hot green chillies, finely chopped

1 teaspoon ground cumin

large handful of chopped coriander leaves

juice of 2 limes

salt and freshly ground black pepper to taste

2 handfuls of pumpkin seeds

Combine all the ingredients, except the pumpkin seeds. Pour into a bowl and chill in the fridge.

Dry roast the pumpkin seeds in a small frying pan until golden, add a little salt and then sprinkle over the salsa just before serving.

GUATEMALAN BREAKFAST

The dishes eaten at breakfast in Guatemala have the same names as the Mexican equivalents; however, they are completely different in flavour. They are spread out on the table and eaten buffet style. Of course you don't have eat these dishes only for breakfast: they make a great sociable lunch or dinner.

SALSA

Unlike Mexican salsa, this contains no tomato or tomatillo, and uses carrot and red onion.

4 medium carrots, grated
1 large red onion, cubed
2 garlic cloves, crushed
2 habanero chillies or 2 hot red
   chillies, roughly chopped

large handful of chopped
   coriander leaves
juice of 2 limes
salt to taste
4 dessertspoons olive oil

Left Corn and
Black Bean Salsa
with Toasted
Pumpkin Seeds

Below Antigua,
Guatemala

Place all the ingredients in a food processor and blend until smooth. Chill in the fridge until required.

GUACAMOLE

Fresh basil and celery are mashed with avocado, cayenne pepper and lime juice.

3 ripe Hass avocados
4 celery sticks, diced
handful of basil leaves, chopped
2 garlic cloves, crushed

juice of 2 limes
¼ teaspoon cayenne pepper
salt to taste

Scoop the avocado flesh into a bowl and mash with a fork until roughly chopped. Stir in the remaining ingredients and chill until required.

REFRIED BEANS

15oz/425g black turtle beans, soaked
   in water overnight
2 large red onions, cubed
6 cloves garlic, chopped

3oz/90g butter, cut into cubes
4 tablespoons olive oil
salt to taste
coriander leaves, to garnish

Drain and rinse the soaked black beans, place in a saucepan and pour in enough water to just cover the beans. Add the onions, garlic and butter, bring to the boil, cover the pan and gently simmer until the beans are soft and nearly all the water has been absorbed. Allow to cool a little, and then blend in a food processor along with the olive oil and salt to taste until a smooth thick purée forms.

Serve garnished with chopped coriander leaves and a drizzle of olive oil.

SCRAMBLED EGG

10 free-range eggs
small handful of oregano leaves,
   chopped
½ teaspoon allspice

salt and freshly ground black pepper
   to taste
2oz/60g butter
2 garlic cloves, crushed

Lightly beat the eggs in a bowl and stir in the oregano, allspice, and salt and black pepper to taste. Heat the butter in a large heavy-bottomed frying pan. When melted, add the crushed garlic and fry until golden. Add the beaten eggs and stir constantly until the eggs are cooked but still soft, as they will continue cooking when you remove them from the heat. Serve immediately.

SERVING THE BREAKFAST

Arrange the above dishes along with: feta cheese, cut into cubes, sour cream, black and green olives, and flour tortillas, toasted on a griddle or in a heavy frying pan.

At our first breakfast in Guatemala, a tray arrived with some refried beans cooked with garlic butter; scrambled eggs laced with oregano leaves and allspice; a carrot, onion and coriander salsa; some guacamole flavoured with basil, celery and cayenne; cubes of feta cheese, olives and sour cream; and a basketful of warm flour tortillas.

Guatemalan Breakfast

Islands of the

Caribbean

Islands of the Caribbean

While the islands of the Caribbean all have their own favourite and unique cuisines, there are many dishes that seem to turn up in only slightly different styles all around the region. Vegetarian dishes are not usually main meals, so we have adapted some of the typical Caribbean recipes we found by substituting meat or fish with vegetables and tofu; others in this chapter, though, are just as we found them. The islands where we found the most interesting food are Jamaica, Anguilla and Nevis.

Nevis is a small island only 6 x 9 miles/9.5 x 14.5 kilometres and dominated by a volcano that descends from a misty peak through rainforest and tropical palms to a circle of fine beaches. Columbus spotted and named it on his voyage of discovery to the Americas in 1493. Once Nevis was colonized, the fertile soil made fortunes for the owners of its sugar plantations. They built opulent mansions and the island became a popular haunt of high society.

With the abolition of slavery and the decline of the sugar trade, Nevis slipped into international obscurity. Remains of sugar mills are scattered about the island. Fortunately some of the grand plantation houses have been preserved and are now run as inns, providing stylish retreats from which to discover the island's many charms. Most of these are hidden away on the slopes of the volcano in a district known as Gingerland. Some of the recipes in this chapter are based on the meals we enjoyed while staying at these hotels; others are from the simple beach cafés dotted around the island.

Jamaica is a much larger island, with a reputation for being a bit dangerous. Many of the resorts are sold as 'all inclusive', meaning that guests never need to venture beyond the safety of their walls. We stayed in Negril, where danger didn't seem to be a problem, and ate some of the best food of our stay in local cafés and bars. One of these bars was located on top of a high cliff that plunged hundreds of feet down to the sea. Every evening local guys with extremely athletic bodies and long dreadlocks would entertain tourists by diving off the cliffs into the sea.

Anguilla, even smaller than Nevis, is blessed with some of the finest beaches in the Caribbean. There are plenty of upmarket hotels that can afford to import the finest ingredients to cook some excellent Caribbean dishes. Here we found a recipe for the best 'rice and peas' dish we have had anywhere. Beyond the hotels there are few places to eat and little to do; however, people were very friendly, especially when they found out that we were English. Almost everyone we met on the island seemed to have relatives in England and strangely all of them lived in Slough!

Pages 154–155 **Tobago Cayes in the Caribbean**

Right, clockwise from top right **A plantation inn on Nevis; Fig Tree Church on Nevis; Soufrière bay on St Lucia; fishing boats on Nevis; Grand Anse bay, Grenada; Tobago Cayes in the Grenadines**

Cajun spice mix is a popular Creole seasoning, which blackens when cooked in a hot pan. It can be used to season almost anything, but we think it works particularly well with tofu. The spice mix can be made in advance and stored in an airtight jar.

CAJUN BLACKENED TOFU

SERVES 4

14oz/400g tofu
olive oil

For the spice mix
8 cloves
1 teaspoon cumin seeds
1 teaspoon black peppercorns

1 teaspoon yellow mustard seeds
1 teaspoon paprika
1 teaspoon cayenne pepper
1 teaspoon dried oregano
2 teaspoons dried thyme
1 teaspoon salt

Dry roast the cloves, cumin seeds, peppercorns and mustard seeds in a small frying pan until aromatic. Remove from the heat and grind to a powder. Combine with the remaining spice mix ingredients.

Drain the tofu, cut into eight slices and pat dry with kitchen paper. Brush each side with olive oil and then coat with the spice mix. Preheat a griddle pan or thick-based frying pan until really hot, place the tofu in the pan and cook until the spices blacken; then turn and cook other side. Alternatively cook on the barbecue.

Serve with Mango and Ginger Salsa (below) and Pumpkin and Pigeon Pea Salad with Lime and Allspice Dressing (page 160).

MANGO AND GINGER SALSA

Salsas are often served with Caribbean dishes to liven up a meal. They are easy to make and look great on the table. This is a particularly delicious one that we were served in Anguilla.

SERVES 4

1 large mango, peeled and chopped
2in/5cm piece of ginger, peeled
 and grated
1 teaspoon brown sugar

1 dessertspoon tarragon,
 finely chopped
juice of 1 lime

Blend the chopped mango, grated ginger, brown sugar, tarragon and lime juice until smooth but retaining some bite. Store in the fridge until required.

**Cajun Blackened Tofu
with Mango and
Ginger Salsa**

PUMPKIN AND PIGEON PEA SALAD WITH LIME AND ALLSPICE DRESSING

Pigeon peas originated in Africa and are used in many recipes throughout the Caribbean. They are available in Caribbean stores or the ethnic section of good supermarkets; however, if you find them impossible to locate, substitute black eye peas (or kidney beans).

SERVES 4

12oz/350g pumpkin, peeled and cut into cubes

2 tablespoons olive oil

1 large red onion, finely chopped

2 cloves garlic, finely chopped

1 teaspoon ground cumin

14oz/400g tin pigeon peas or black eye peas, drained and rinsed

10oz/300g cooked brown rice

1 red pepper, cut into small cubes

2 celery sticks, cut into small cubes

chopped coriander leaves, to garnish

For the dressing

3 tablespoons lime juice

grated zest of 2 limes

2 tablespoons olive oil

½ teaspoon allspice

5 stems of thyme, finely chopped

salt and freshly ground black pepper to taste

Put the pumpkin in a saucepan of boiling water and simmer until soft, drain and set to one side. Heat 2 tablespoons of the olive oil in a wok. When hot, add the chopped red onion and garlic and sauté until the onion softens; then add the ground cumin, stirring it into the onions. Add the pumpkin and fry until it starts to brown. Remove from the heat, place in a large bowl and add the pigeon peas or black eye peas, cooked brown rice, red pepper and celery.

Make the dressing by whisking together the lime juice and grated zest, the remaining 2 tablespoons of the olive oil, allspice, chopped thyme, salt and freshly ground black pepper. Pour over the salad and combine well.

You can either eat the salad warm or chill it in the fridge for 30 minutes. Serve garnished with chopped coriander leaves.

A fishing boat on Pinney's beach, Nevis

COU-COU

Cou-cou is the Caribbean version of polenta, made from cornmeal and okra. It is used as a side dish to any meal.

SERVES 4

1½ pints/750ml water	6fl oz/175ml coconut milk
1 teaspoon salt	good dash of Tabasco
8oz/225g okra, sliced into	½ teaspoon freshly ground
½in/1cm rounds	black pepper
6oz/175g cornmeal or fine polenta	2 tablespoons butter, softened

Bring the water and salt to boil in a heavy saucepan, add the okra and boil for 10 minutes with the lid on; then remove the okra with a slotted spoon and keep to one side. Slowly pour in the cornmeal or fine polenta, stirring constantly with a whisk. Whisk in the coconut milk, and then add the okra. Stir constantly until a thick mixture forms. Add the Tabasco and the freshly ground black pepper. Pour the cou-cou into a bowl and spread the butter on top. Serve immediately.

Horse riding in
Jamaica

SEASONING-UP BARBECUE MARINADE

This also makes a good marinade for ingredients to be cooked under the grill or in the oven.

1 large onion, roughly chopped	1 teaspoon paprika
3 garlic cloves, roughly chopped	½ teaspoon ground cloves
½–1 Scotch bonnet chilli, roughly chopped	½ teaspoon freshly ground black pepper
1 tablespoon chopped marjoram	3 tablespoons lime juice
1 tablespoon chopped thyme	3 tablespoons sunflower oil
1 tablespoon chopped chives	salt to taste

Place all the ingredients in a food processor and blend until smooth. The marinade can be stored in a jar in the fridge until needed.

To serve, brush the marinade over your favourite barbecue ingredients – we suggest sweet corn cobs, thick-cut slices of sweet potato or tofu. Allow to marinate for 1 hour before cooking on the barbecue or under a hot grill, or baking in the oven. Serve with Papaya and Mango Salsa (page 165).

Traditionally known as callaloo, this dish is usually made with callaloo leaves, but we find them hard to get, so we use spinach instead.

SPINACH WITH COCONUT MILK, THYME AND CHIVES

SERVES 4

1oz/30g butter
1 large onion, diced
2 garlic cloves, chopped
1lb/450g peeled and cubed pumpkin
1 green pepper, cut into cubes
4oz/115g okra, cut into ½in/1cm slices
1 tablespoon chopped thyme

8floz/250ml vegetable stock
10oz/300g spinach, washed, stems removed and roughly chopped
14fl oz/400ml coconut milk
1 tablespoon chopped chives
salt and freshly ground black pepper to taste

Melt the butter in a large saucepan, add the onion and garlic, and sauté until the onion is soft. Add the pumpkin, green pepper and okra, and fry until the pumpkin starts to soften. Add the thyme and vegetable stock, bring to the boil, cover with a lid and simmer for 10 minutes. Add the spinach, and when it has wilted down, add the coconut milk and chives. Gently simmer for a further 10 minutes, taking care not to boil the coconut milk as it will split. Finally add salt and freshly ground black pepper to taste.

JAMAICAN JERK TOFU

1 onion, roughly chopped

1 Scotch bonnet chilli, chopped

2 garlic cloves, chopped

1in/2.5cm piece of ginger, peeled
  and grated

2 tablespoons honey

2 tablespoons sunflower oil

3 tablespoons soy sauce

2 tablespoons red wine vinegar

2 teaspoons dried thyme

1 teaspoon allspice

1 teaspoon ground cinnamon

1 teaspoon ground cloves

freshly ground black pepper to taste

1lb 2oz/500g tofu

Blend all the ingredients except the tofu in a food processor until smooth. Drain the tofu, pat it dry with kitchen paper and cut into 12 pieces. Coat with the jerk sauce and allow to marinate for half an hour. Cook on a barbecue or under a hot grill until brown on both sides. Any remaining sauce can be kept in the fridge, in a jar with a tight-fitting lid, until next time. Serve with Negril Tomato Catch-up (opposite) and Caribbean Rice and Peas (below).

CARIBBEAN RICE AND PEAS

Peas and rice are served all over the Caribbean and everyone has their own special recipe. This recipe, which we found in Jamaica, also works well with black eye peas.

12oz/350g basmati rice

1 large onion, finely chopped

2 garlic cloves, finely chopped

1 tablespoon chopped thyme

1 teaspoon salt

½ teaspoon freshly ground black pepper

1 dessertspoon honey

1 teacup kidney beans, soaked
  overnight and cooked until soft, or
  14oz/400g tin, rinsed

14fl oz/400ml coconut milk

8fl oz/250ml water

chopped coriander leaves, to garnish

Rinse the rice until the water runs clear, and then place in a saucepan with a tight-fitting lid. Add the onion, garlic, thyme, salt, pepper, honey and kidney beans. Add the coconut milk and water, cover with the lid and bring to the boil; then reduce the heat to a minimum and gently cook until the rice is tender, adding more water if necessary. Serve garnished with chopped coriander leaves.

Jerk seasoning is probably the most famous taste to come out of Jamaica. It is a sweet and spicy marinade, and stalls selling it can be found all over the island, grilling meat on barbecues made out of huge oil drums cut in half. The smell is irresistible. We like it as a marinade for tofu and it works both on the barbecue in summer or under the grill

PAPAYA AND MANGO SALSA

1 medium mango, peeled and cut
  into small cubes
1 papaya, peeled, deseeded and cut
  into small cubes
1 red pepper, cut into small cubes

1 red chilli, finely chopped
juice of 1 lime
¼ teaspoon grated nutmeg
1 tablespoon chopped marjoram

Combine all the ingredients and chill in the fridge for 1 hour before serving.

NEGRIL TOMATO CATCH-UP

This spicy Caribbean version of tomato ketchup is a good accompaniment to any Caribbean meal. It can be made in advance and kept in a jar in the fridge.

1lb 4oz/565g ripe tomatoes
2 tablespoons sunflower oil
1 medium onion, finely chopped
2 garlic cloves, finely chopped
2 green chillies, finely chopped
½ teaspoon ground ginger
1 teaspoon ground coriander
½ teaspoon ground cinnamon

½ teaspoon ground cloves
½ teaspoon ground nutmeg
1 teaspoon paprika
½ teaspoon ground mace
½ teaspoon salt
¼ teaspoon freshly ground black pepper
1 dessertspoon honey

Chop the tomatoes in a blender and set to one side. Heat the oil in a saucepan. When hot, add the onion and garlic and gently fry until the onion is soft but not brown. Add the chopped chillies and the spices, and turn in the oil for 1 minute or so. Add the chopped tomatoes, salt, pepper and honey and bring to the boil; then reduce the heat and gently simmer, uncovered, for 15 minutes until the tomatoes have reduced and the catch-up coats the back of a spoon.

MARINATED BUTTERNUT SQUASH AND SWEET PEPPERS WITH HOT TOMATO SAUCE

In this dish the peppers and butternut squash are marinated and cooked on the barbecue or under the grill and then served with a hot, spicy tomato sauce.

1lb/450g butternut squash, peeled and cut into ¾in/2cm chunks

2 large red onions, cut into ¾in/2cm chunks

3 red peppers, cut into ¾in/2cm cubes

For the marinade

1 tablespoon chopped thyme

1 tablespoon chopped chives

2 tablespoons fresh lime juice

1 tablespoon soy sauce

3 tablespoons olive oil

1 dessertspoon honey

For the tomato sauce

2 tablespoons sunflower oil

1 large onion, diced

2 garlic cloves, finely chopped

½–1 Scotch bonnet chilli, finely chopped

4oz/115g okra pods, chopped in ½in/1cm rounds

14oz/400g ripe tomatoes, cut into cubes

3 bay leaves

1 tablespoon chopped thyme

1 tablespoon lime juice

salt and black pepper to taste

Parboil the squash in a saucepan of boiling water until it is just starting to soften but is still firm. Drain and place in a large bowl with the onions, peppers and marinade ingredients. Stir well to coat all the vegetables with the marinade and set to one side for 1 hour.

Meanwhile make the tomato sauce. Heat the sunflower oil in a saucepan. When hot, add the onion, garlic, chilli and okra, and gently fry until soft. Add the tomatoes, bay leaves, thyme and lime juice, and bring to the boil; cover the pan and simmer until the sauce has reduced and the oil returns. Add salt and black pepper to taste.

Skewer the onions, peppers and butternut squash and cook either on the barbecue or under a hot grill until brown on all sides. Any remaining marinade can be added to the tomato sauce and heated through.

Serve the skewers topped with the sauce, with rice on the side.

Marinated Butternut Squash and Sweet Peppers with Hot Tomato Sauce

CARIBBEAN PEPPERPOT

Pepperpot is one of the Caribbean's most famous dishes. It can be served as a soup or as a meal in a bowl. It is usually made with whatever vegetables are in season.

3 tablespoons sunflower oil

1 large onion, diced

4 garlic cloves, finely chopped

½–1 Scotch bonnet chilli, finely chopped

1 large red-skinned sweet potato, peeled and cut into chunks

20 okra pods, sliced in ½in/1cm rounds

1 tablespoon chopped thyme

1 teaspoon allspice

1 teaspoon ground cloves

1 teaspoon ground cinnamon

½ teaspoon ground nutmeg

½ teaspoon ground mace

½ teaspoon ground black pepper

10oz/300g kale, washed with stems removed and roughly chopped

1 pint/500ml vegetable stock

6oz/175g spinach leaves, washed, stems removed and roughly chopped

1 tablespoon chopped chives

1 tablespoon chopped marjoram

4 spring onions, sliced

salt to taste

Heat the oil in a large saucepan. When hot, add the onion, garlic and chilli, and sauté until the onion is soft. Add the sweet potato and okra, and cook until the okra starts to brown, stirring to prevent the okra from sticking. Stir the thyme and spices into the pan; then add the kale, stock and enough water to cover the vegetables. Bring to the boil, cover the pan and reduce the heat, and simmer until the sweet potato is just soft. Add the spinach, chives, marjoram, spring onions and salt to taste, and cook for a further 5 minutes.

Ladle into bowls and serve immediately.

Seaside fun in Jamaica

Venice

Venice

Venice is, of course, unique. The cuisine of Venice is not particularly unique; however, the way it is purchased, prepared and consumed is, as it almost always involves a journey on, along or over a canal. Venetian markets are even more spectacular and seductive than any others in Italy because they are always on a canal; produce, traders and customers all arrive and leave by boat. There are the canalside restaurants, mostly tourist traps now, selling their location rather than good food for outrageous prices; and even the little cafés down the back streets where the locals go are reached by a series of bridges and canal crossings.

On previous visits to Venice we had been frustrated by seeing all the wonderful produce on sale in the markets: we could not buy or taste it, as all we had was a room in a hotel. We found many excellent antipasti dishes in the bars and cafés which could be enjoyed at very reasonable prices standing at the counter with a tumbler of house wine; however, most of our attempts to go out and eat a proper meal ended in little choice and large bills.

This time we rented an apartment just off the Grand Canal for a week and had a very different experience. Even getting there was more fun, as we took a water taxi from the airport to what would for the next week be the landing place nearest our house, and then walked down narrow lanes along lesser canals until we found our front door.

Living in a neighbourhood among Venetians, going out in the morning to buy fresh bread and milk, stopping at the same bar every day for a coffee on the way back and coming home laden with shopping from the Rialto market to begin cooking a meal was so much more fun than staying in an overpriced room in another hotel.

As it was June, the day started early enough to get up every morning and wander around the city for a couple of hours before any other tourists hit the streets or clogged the canals in crocodiles of gondolas. It was the perfect time to get hopelessly lost and soak up the atmosphere, knowing that eventually we would end up at a vaporetto stop and be taken home by one of the water buses just as they began to fill up with morning commuters.

The Rialto market was just three stops from our apartment on the vaporetto. We never tired of going there and looking for new ingredients.

The recipes here are based on the best antipasti dishes we discovered at the bar of our favourite café and recreated in the kitchen of the apartment.

Pages 170–171 **Venice lagoon at dusk**

Right, clockwise from top right **Piazzetta San Marco; gondoliers on a bridge; the Venice regatta; a view from Palazzo Contarini**

CAVOLO NERO AND OYSTER MUSHROOMS WITH CHILLI, GARLIC AND PARMESAN

1lb 2oz/500g cavolo nero

4 tablespoons olive oil

4 garlic cloves, finely chopped

2 red onions, finely sliced

8oz/225g oyster mushrooms, sliced

3 red chillies, deseeded and thinly sliced

8fl oz/250ml vegetable stock

salt and freshly ground black pepper to taste

freshly grated Parmesan cheese, as much or as little as desired, to serve

Cavolo nero is an Italian version of cabbage, but much more glamorous. It is dark green and comes in bunches of long leaves. We think this is the best way to serve it and it is a good accompaniment to Creamy Polenta with Mascarpone and Fresh Herbs (right).

Wash and trim the thick stalks of the cavolo nero, and cut into 1in/2.5cm slices. Heat the olive oil in a wok. When hot, add the garlic, red onions, oyster mushrooms and chillies, and fry until soft. Add the cavolo nero and fry for 5 minutes or so, stirring regularly. Pour in the stock, cover the pan, reduce the heat and simmer until almost all the liquid has been absorbed. Finally add salt and freshly ground black pepper to taste.

Turn out into a bowl and take to the table. Allow everyone to sprinkle over as much Parmesan as they desire.

The Palazzo Contarini

POLENTA

Polenta is a staple for Venetians. Made from ground corn, it is eaten either soft, like mashed potato, or set and grilled with salad and vegetables. Both ways are delicious.

CREAMY POLENTA WITH MASCARPONE AND FRESH HERBS

Mascarpone is an Italian cream cheese with a high cream content that is used in both savoury and sweet recipes. You can use any fresh chopped herbs in this recipe; we like to use marjoram and basil. Serve this polenta immediately, as if you leave it too long it will start to set.

1¾ pints / 1 litre water	handful of chopped marjoram leaves
6oz / 175g fine polenta	handful of chopped basil leaves
7oz / 200g mascarpone cheese	salt and freshly ground black pepper
2oz / 60g butter	grated Parmesan cheese and olive oil,
3 tablespoons grated Parmesan cheese	to serve

Bring the water to the boil in a heavy-bottomed pan and gradually pour in the polenta, whisking constantly to prevent lumps from forming. Reduce the heat to a minimum and gently simmer for about 12 minutes, until the polenta becomes the consistency of mashed potato. Make sure that you keep stirring to prevent the polenta sticking. Stir in the mascarpone, butter, grated Parmesan, chopped herbs, salt and freshly ground black pepper.

Serve immediately, with more grated Parmesan sprinkled over it and drizzled with olive oil, with Cavolo Nero and Oyster Mushrooms with Chilli, Garlic and Parmesan (opposite).

GRILLED POLENTA WITH MELTED GORGONZOLA AND PEAR, WALNUT AND ROCKET SALAD

This polenta needs a couple of hours to set. We often make it the day before and leave it in the fridge overnight.

1¾ pints/1 litre water
6oz/175g fine polenta
2oz/60g butter
2 tablespoons olive oil
salt and freshly ground black pepper
  to taste

6oz/175g Gorgonzola cheese, cut
  into thin slices
3 large handfuls rocket leaves
3 large pears, peeled, cored and
  thinly sliced
large handful walnut halves
olive oil and balsamic vinegar, to serve

Make the polenta, as described on page 175, and then stir in the butter, olive oil, salt and black pepper. Cook for a further 10 minutes, stirring constantly, and then turn out into a greased 10 × 10in/25 × 25cm dish. Allow to cool and then place in the fridge for a couple of hours.

When the polenta is ready to serve, cut it into slices, brush each side with a little olive oil, and grill on each side or fry in a griddle pan until golden brown.

Serve immediately, topped with the Gorgonzola slices, garnished with the rocket leaves, sliced pears and walnuts, and drizzled with olive oil and balsamic vinegar.

Grilled Polenta with Melted Gorgonzola and Pear, Walnut and Rocket Salad

ANTIPASTI

Antipasti are how Venetians start a meal. If you want to eat cheaply in Venice, it is always a good option to order a few of these dishes at the bar, as they can be quite filling and there are always lots of vegetarian options. Serve a selection of dishes with crusty bread.

COURGETTES AND FENNEL WITH A GREMOLITA OF LEMON ZEST AND FRESH HERBS

olive oil

4 garlic cloves, finely chopped

3 medium fennel bulbs, sliced thinly
   lengthways (do not remove the
   core, so that the slices hold together)

5 large courgettes, sliced lengthways

lemon juice to taste

salt and freshly ground black pepper
   to taste

For the gremolita

handful of finely chopped
   flat-leaf parsley

small handful of finely chopped sage

grated zest of 4 large unwaxed lemons

3 garlic cloves, crushed

salt and freshly ground black pepper
   to taste

Heat a good splash of olive oil in a large frying pan. When hot, add half the garlic, fry until golden and then lay the fennel in the bottom of the pan (you may need to do this in two batches if your pan isn't big enough) and continue frying until soft and brown on both sides. Carefully remove from the pan and lay out on a large platter. Add another good splash of olive oil to the frying pan. When hot, repeat the process with the courgettes. Drizzle the vegetables with a little lemon juice and season to taste.

   Make the gremolita by combining all the ingredients. Sprinkle over the fennel and courgette platter.

Courgettes and Fennel with a Gremolita of Lemon Zest and Fresh Herbs

Pages 178–179, clockwise from top right Paint powder in an art shop; the entrance to the Arsenale; a Venetian doorway; artichokes in the Rialto market; walking flowers; Piazza San Marco at dawn; courgette flowers

Salsa verde is a herb and caper sauce that can also be served as a dressing for grilled vegetables. The aubergine salad can either be made in advance and chilled or served warm.

AUBERGINE SALAD WITH PINE NUTS AND SALSA VERDE

handful of pine nuts
5 tablespoons olive oil
1 large red onion, finely chopped
5 celery sticks, cubed
4 garlic cloves, finely chopped
1½lb/750g aubergines, cubed
squeeze of lemon juice
salt and freshly ground black pepper
3 tablespoons finely chopped parsley

For the salsa verde
handful of chopped flat-leaf parsley
handful of chopped basil leaves
2 garlic cloves, crushed
2 tablespoons salted capers, washed
    to remove the salt
4 tablespoons olive oil
grated zest of 1 lemon
juice of ½ a lemon
freshly ground black pepper to taste

Blend all the salsa verde ingredients in a food processor until smooth. Dry roast the pine nuts in a small frying pan until golden. Set both salsa verde and pine nuts to one side while you make the salad.

Heat the olive oil in a wok. When hot, add the sliced red onion, celery and garlic, and fry until soft. Add the cubed aubergines, sprinkle with a little salt and fry until the aubergines are soft. Add a good squeeze of lemon juice, and salt and pepper to taste. Turn out on to a dish, spoon over the salsa verde and sprinkle over the dry roasted pine nuts. Garnish with the parsley.

BUTTER BEAN, HERB AND CAPER SALAD

1lb 2oz/500g cooked butter beans
3 plum tomatoes, diced
1 red onion, finely chopped
1 garlic clove, crushed
2 tablespoons salted capers, washed
    to remove the salt

handful of pitted black olives, chopped
large handful of chopped oregano leaves
good squeeze of lemon juice
good drizzle of olive oil
freshly ground black pepper

Combine all the ingredients and chill in the fridge until ready to serve.

Puddings

In the first book we included only one pudding recipe, for French chocolate cake, which is the most asked-for recipe of all the things we make. However, so many customers have asked us to put more in the next book that we have included the next ten most popular here.

ORANGE, DATE AND CINNAMON FRUIT SALAD

This simple, delicious fruit salad is popular in Morocco. It is a great way to finish a meal.

5 medium oranges, peeled and
    thinly sliced
12 fresh dates, stoned and
    thinly sliced

handful of flaked almonds
1 tablespoon orange flower water
ground cinnamon to taste
natural yoghurt, to serve

Lay the oranges on a large platter and sprinkle over the dates, flaked almonds, orange flower water and cinnamon to taste. Serve with natural yoghurt.

TROPICAL FRUIT PLATTER WITH CHAT MASALA

In India fruit is served sprinkled with a spice mix called chat masala, a delicious sweet and savoury combination. You can use any fruit you have in the fruit bowl, but tropical fruit works particularly well. Make the chat masala in advance and store it in an airtight container until required.

tropical fruit, such as pineapple,
    papaya, mango, melon, star fruit or
    chikoo, peeled, deseeded and cut
    into slices
good squeeze of lime juice
2 limes, cut into wedges, to garnish

For the chat masala
2 teaspoons black peppercorns
2 teaspoons cumin seeds
2 teaspoons dried pomegranate seeds
1 teaspoon caraway seeds
2 teaspoons ground mango powder
½ teaspoon ground chilli
1 teaspoon garam masala
salt to taste

Dry roast the pepper, cumin, pomegranate and caraway seeds in a small frying pan until aromatic. Allow to cool a little and then grind to a powder. Combine with the remaining ingredients. Store in an airtight jar.

Arrange the fruit slices on a large platter, squeeze over a good splash of lime juice and garnish with the lime wedges. Just before serving, sprinkle over the chat masala to taste.

Orange, Date and
Cinnamon Fruit Salad

POMEGRANATE GRANITA

Granita is a water ice, thought to have been introduced to Venice when Marco Polo returned from his travels in China. Pomegranate syrup is available in Middle Eastern stores. If you find it impossible to buy, experiment with puréed soft fruit or juice of your choice. Strawberries work well (use approximately 1lb/500g).

5fl oz/150ml pomegranate syrup
6oz/175g castor sugar
1 pint/500ml water

juice of 2 limes
sliced strawberries, to garnish

Blend all the ingredients in a food processor until the castor sugar has dissolved. Pour into a plastic container and place in the freezer.

After 1 hour, remove from the freezer and break up, with a fork, any ice crystals that have formed; this is to prevent the granita from becoming one solid block. Repeat every hour or so, until all the liquid has frozen – it should have the consistency of crushed ice. Store in the freezer until required. We serve it piled into glasses topped with sliced strawberries or, at home, with a slug of vodka.

CHILLI AND LIME ICE CREAM

Chillies work really well in desserts, particularly in this ice cream. The sugar and cream perfectly balance the heat of the chilli.

grated zest of 2 limes
juice of 2 limes
2 red chillies, roughly chopped
7oz/200g castor sugar

3fl oz/100ml water
1 pint/500ml double cream
lime slices or star fruit, to garnish

Blend the lime zest, lime juice, chillies, sugar and water in a food processor until the chilli is finely chopped and the sugar has dissolved. Lightly whip the cream until sloppy, stir in the chilli and lime mix and then pour into a plastic container. Place in the freezer.

After 1 hour, remove from the freezer and break up, with a fork, any ice crystals that have formed. Repeat every hour or so until the cream has completely frozen.

Serve piled into glasses and garnished with lime slices.

PISTACHIO KULFI

Brought to India by the Mughals, kulfi is basically ice cream, but it differs in flavour and texture as it is made with reduced milk. It is traditionally made in cone-shaped receptacles; however, as these are quite hard to buy, we make them in tart trays and pile three on top of each other with sliced fruit in between. Kulfi is usually very sweet but we have cut down the sugar content so that you can taste all the different flavours.

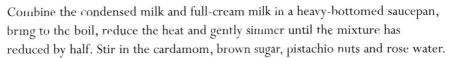

1lb/450g condensed milk
1 pint/500ml full-cream milk
½ teaspoon ground cardamom
3 dessertspoons brown sugar

1oz/30g pistachio nuts, ground
1 dessertspoon rose water
sliced strawberries and physalis, to
garnish

Combine the condensed milk and full-cream milk in a heavy-bottomed saucepan, bring to the boil, reduce the heat and gently simmer until the mixture has reduced by half. Stir in the cardamom, brown sugar, pistachio nuts and rose water.

Meanwhile prepare your tart trays – you will need two – by lining them with cling film. Pour the kulfi mixture into a jug and carefully pour into the individual segments of the tart trays. Place in the freezer overnight; then remove from the freezer and lift the cling film away from the tray – the kulfi will come away with it. Place the frozen kulfi in a plastic tub and store in the freezer until required.

Serve piled three high, garnished with sliced strawberries and physalis.

Above Chilli and Lime Ice Cream; *below* Pistachio Kulfi

APPLE, DATE AND CINNAMON CAKE

We have a lot of demand for vegan cakes in the café, so we created this cake, which non-vegans enjoy as well.

4oz/115g dairy-free margarine
4oz/115g brown sugar
1fl oz/30ml sunflower oil
2fl oz/60ml soya milk
7oz/200g self-raising flour
1 teaspoon baking powder
1 heaped dessertspoon
   ground cinnamon

½ teaspoon salt
3 red apples, grated
handful of dates, finely chopped
handful of mixed nuts, chopped
brown sugar
fresh fig slices and soya or whipped
   double cream, to serve

Preheat the oven to 350°F/180°C.

Blend the margarine and brown sugar in a mixer (or with a hand whisk) until creamy. While still mixing, add the oil, followed by the soya milk, and mix until well incorporated. Reduce the speed of the mixer and gradually add the self-raising flour, baking powder, cinnamon and salt. Add the grated apple and chopped dates, and pour into a greased 9in/23cm loose-bottomed cake tin. Sprinkle the chopped nuts and a little brown sugar over the top of the cake, and gently press into the mixture. Place in the oven and bake for 1 hour 15 minutes or until a knife comes out clean.

Allow to cool and serve with fresh fig slices and soya or whipped cream.

Apple, Date and Cinnamon Cake

CARROT CAKE

This is a recipe my mother gave me. It is so popular with one of our customers, who has moved to Scotland, that when her husband is in town he has to take a piece back to her in Scotland. We have also developed a vegan version, which is printed below.

7oz/200g brown sugar	2 medium free-range eggs
4fl oz/125ml sunflower oil	6oz/175g self-raising flour
1 dessertspoon ground cinnamon	2 medium carrots, grated
½ teaspoon salt	handful of sultanas

Preheat the oven to 375°F/190°C.

Blend the sugar, oil, cinnamon, salt and eggs in a mixer, or using a hand whisk, until creamy. Reduce the speed and gradually stir in the flour; when it is well combined add the grated carrot and sultanas. Pour the mixture into a loaf tin, lined with baking paper, and bake in the oven for 1 hour 15 minutes or until a knife inserted comes out clean, as it can sometimes take longer. Allow to cool a little and then remove from the tin.

CARROT CAKE (VEGAN VERSION)

7oz/200g brown sugar	8oz/225g self-raising flour
6fl oz/175ml sunflower oil	1 teaspoon baking powder
2½fl oz/75ml soya milk	2 medium carrots, grated
1 dessertspoon ground cinnamon	handful of sultanas
½ teaspoon salt	

Make the cake as described above, blending the sugar, oil, soya milk, cinnamon and salt, and then adding the self-raising flour and baking powder, followed by the carrots and sultanas.

MANGO AND PASSION FRUIT CHEESECAKE

7oz/200g digestive or ginger biscuits,
    roughly broken
2oz/60g butter, melted
7oz/200g cream cheese
4 free-range eggs
7oz/200g castor sugar
4 heaped tablespoons natural yoghurt

1 mango, peeled and grated
2 passion fruit, passed through a sieve
    to remove the pips
grated zest of 2 limes
juice of 2 limes
double cream and extra passion fruit,
    to serve

Preheat the oven to 350°F/180°C.

Blend the broken biscuits in a food processor until finely chopped. Add the melted butter and turn out into a greased, loose-bottomed 9in/23cm cake tin. Press into the bottom.

Make the filling by blending the cream cheese, eggs, sugar and yoghurt until smooth and creamy. Stir in the mango, sieved passion fruit, lime zest and juice, and pour into the cake tin. Place in the oven for 1 hour 15 minutes.

The cheesecake is cooked when there is a slight wobble when you shake the cake tin. Turn off the oven and cut around the edge of the cheesecake, but leave the cheesecake in the oven for a further 10 minutes. This should prevent it from cracking.

Serve with whipped double cream and passion fruit scooped over the top.

GUATEMALAN FLAN

In this dish, popular throughout the whole of Latin America, custard is baked over caramel to make a pudding similar to crème caramel, the ultimate comfort food. You will need a flan dish big enough to hold 2 pints/1 litre of milk.

7oz/200g castor sugar

1 tablespoon water

5 free-range eggs

2 pints/1 litre full-fat milk

1 vanilla pod, slit down the middle lengthwise

4in/10cm piece of cinnamon

Preheat the oven to 325°F/170°C.

Place half the sugar and the water in a heavy-bottomed pan, and heat on a medium heat until the sugar melts. Reduce the heat and simmer, stirring regularly, until the sugar becomes like caramel. Pour into your flan dish and spread over the bottom. Set to one side while you make the custard.

Break the eggs into a large bowl and beat with a whisk until creamy. Place the milk, vanilla pod, cinnamon and remaining sugar in a saucepan. Bring to the boil, reduce the heat and gently simmer for a couple of minutes. Remove from the heat and allow to cool a little.

Pull out the vanilla pod and cinnamon stick, and pour the milk into the beaten eggs, whisking constantly. Pour the custard into the flan dish. Place the flan dish into a bain marie, made by filling a baking tray with enough water to come halfway up the side of the flan dish. Carefully place in the oven and bake for about 50 minutes, until the custard has set.

Allow the flan to cool before spooning into dishes and serving.

Index